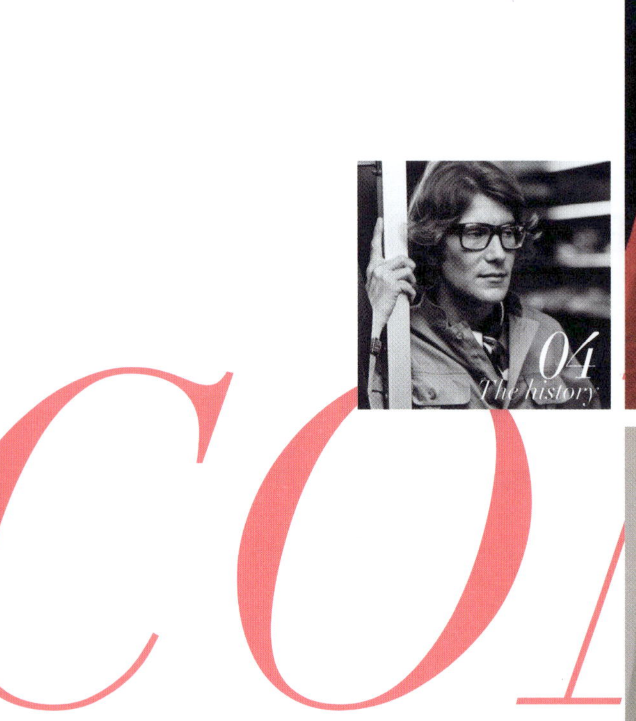

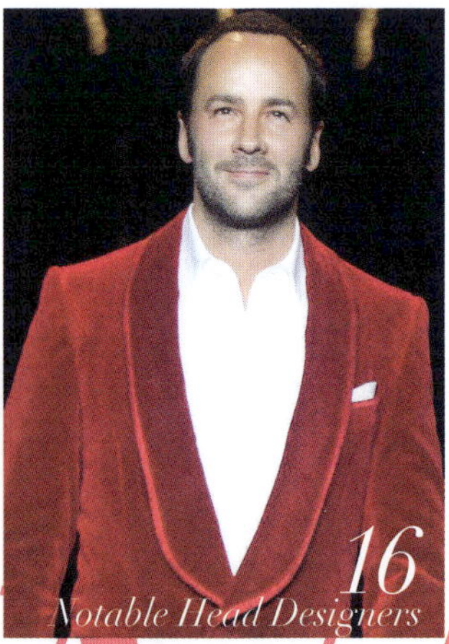

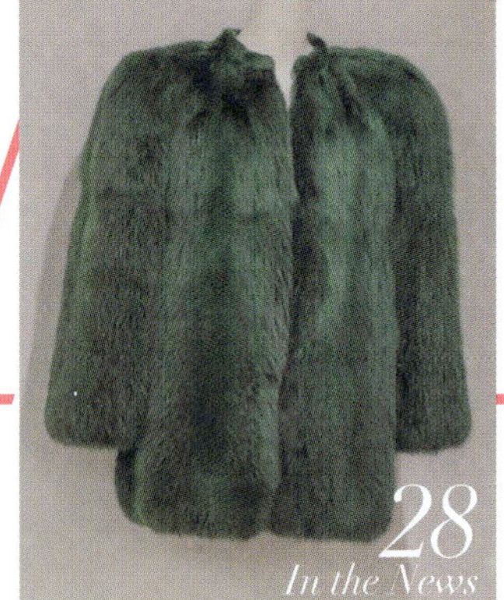

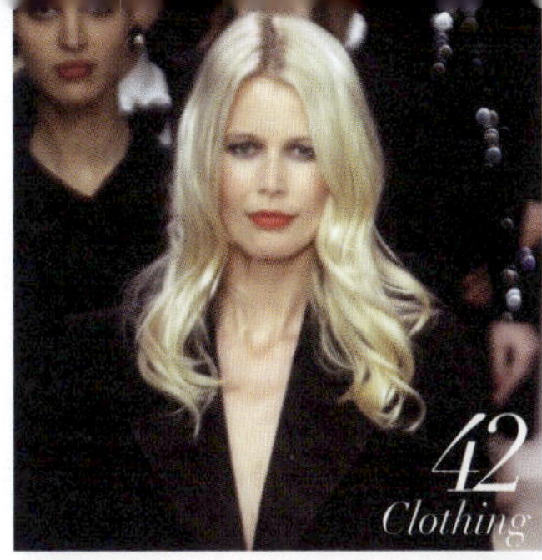

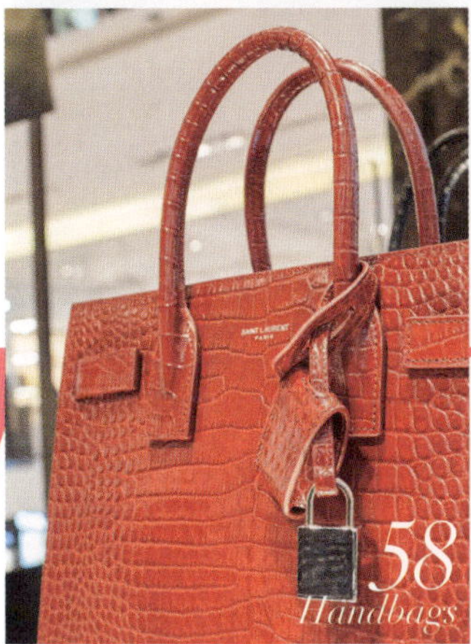

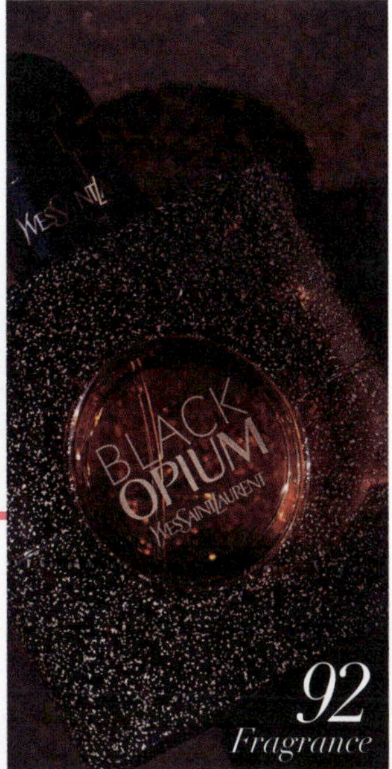
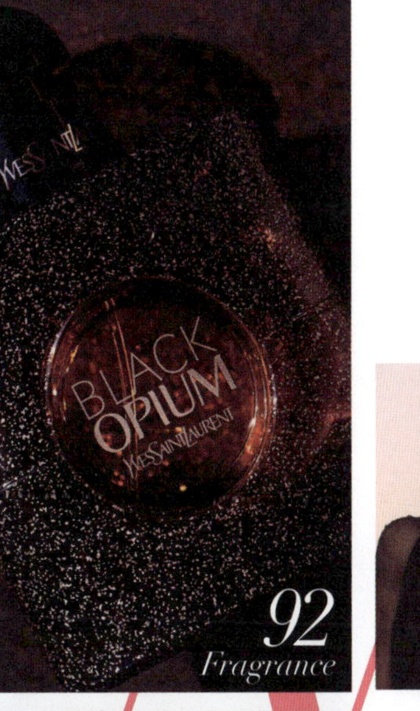
BLACK
OPIUM
YVESSAINTLAURENT

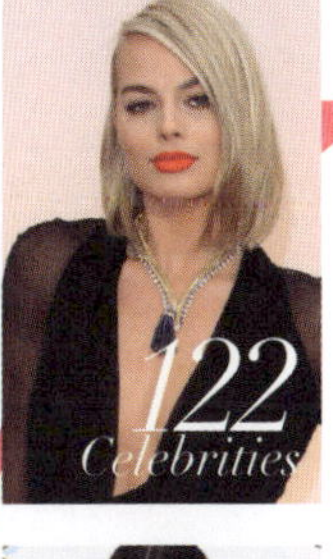

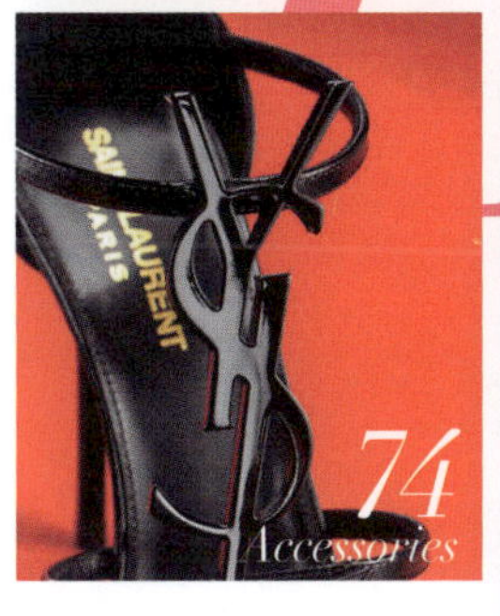
SAINT LAURENT
PARIS

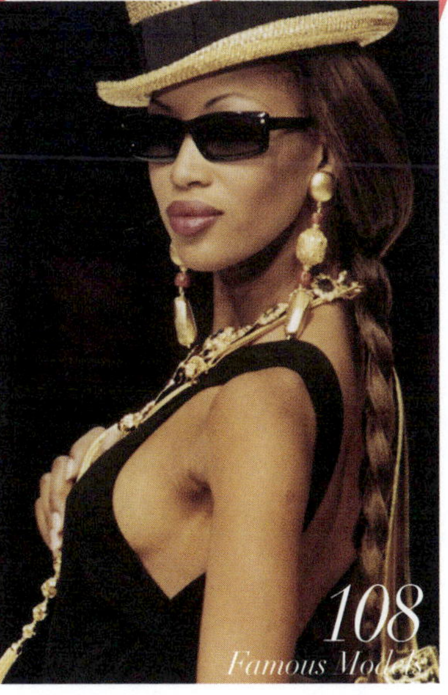

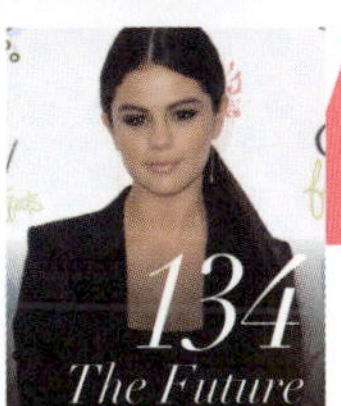

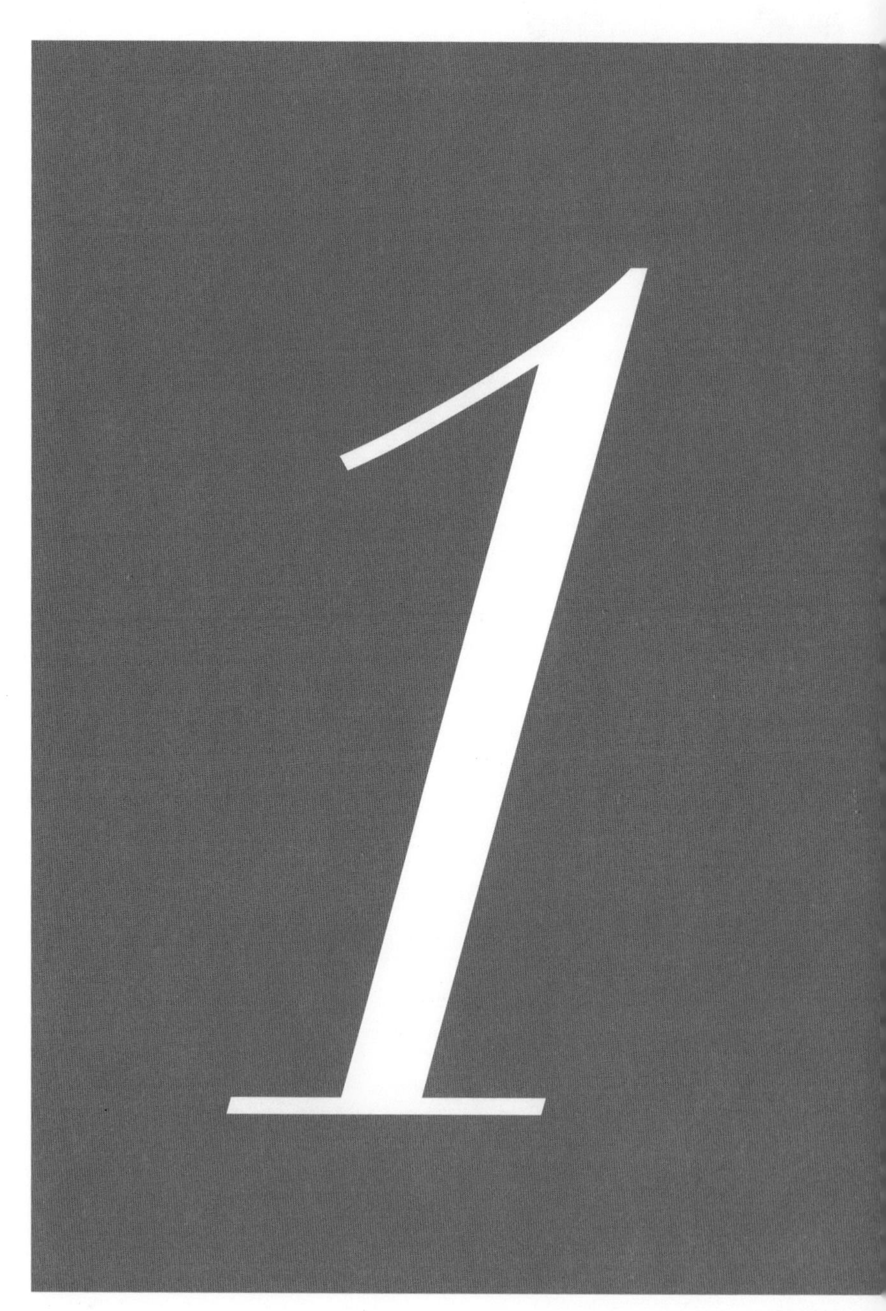

The Beginning of YVES SAINT LAURENT

The History

THE LUXURY FASHION HOUSE OF YVES SAINT LAURENT is sometimes simply referred to as Saint Laurent or YSL. No matter what you call this historic fashion brand, it has left a significant legacy in the world of fashion, accessories, and beauty.

This renowned label came from the mind of one man, Yves Saint Laurent, in 1962. Yves Henri Donat Mathieu-Saint-Laurent was born in 1936 in Oran, Algeria. His parents were from France, and he grew up on the idyllic shores of the Mediterranean alongside his two little sisters. When he was a teenager, he started designing and making dresses for his mother and sisters.

From a very young age, it was clear that Yves was destined to be a designer. After he graduated from high school, Yves moved to Paris and attended a prestigious design school where his work was far superior to that of his classmates. People in the fashion world started to take notice, and the editor of French Vogue introduced Yves to a very important French fashion designer, Christian Dior, who would eventually become Yves' mentor and give him his first real job in 1955. Christian immediately saw the impressive talent that Yves had and made him his assistant. Even though Yves started out performing only basic tasks for the House of Dior, Christian eventually let him create couture dresses from his amazing sketches. Yves always said that Christian taught him everything he knew about art and design. Christian's influence was very important to Yves, and he did everything he could to soak in everything Christian wanted to teach him.

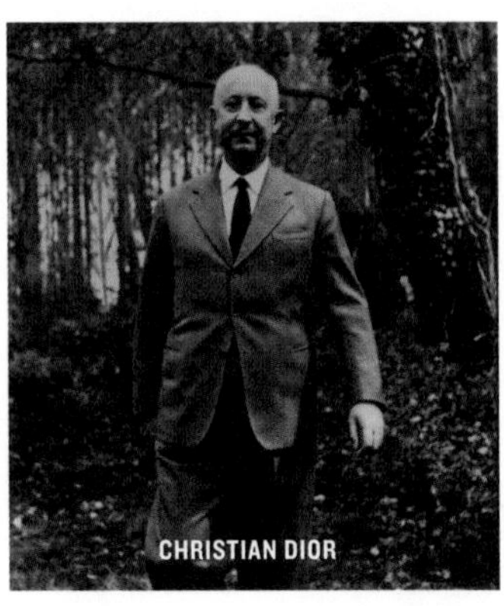
CHRISTIAN DIOR

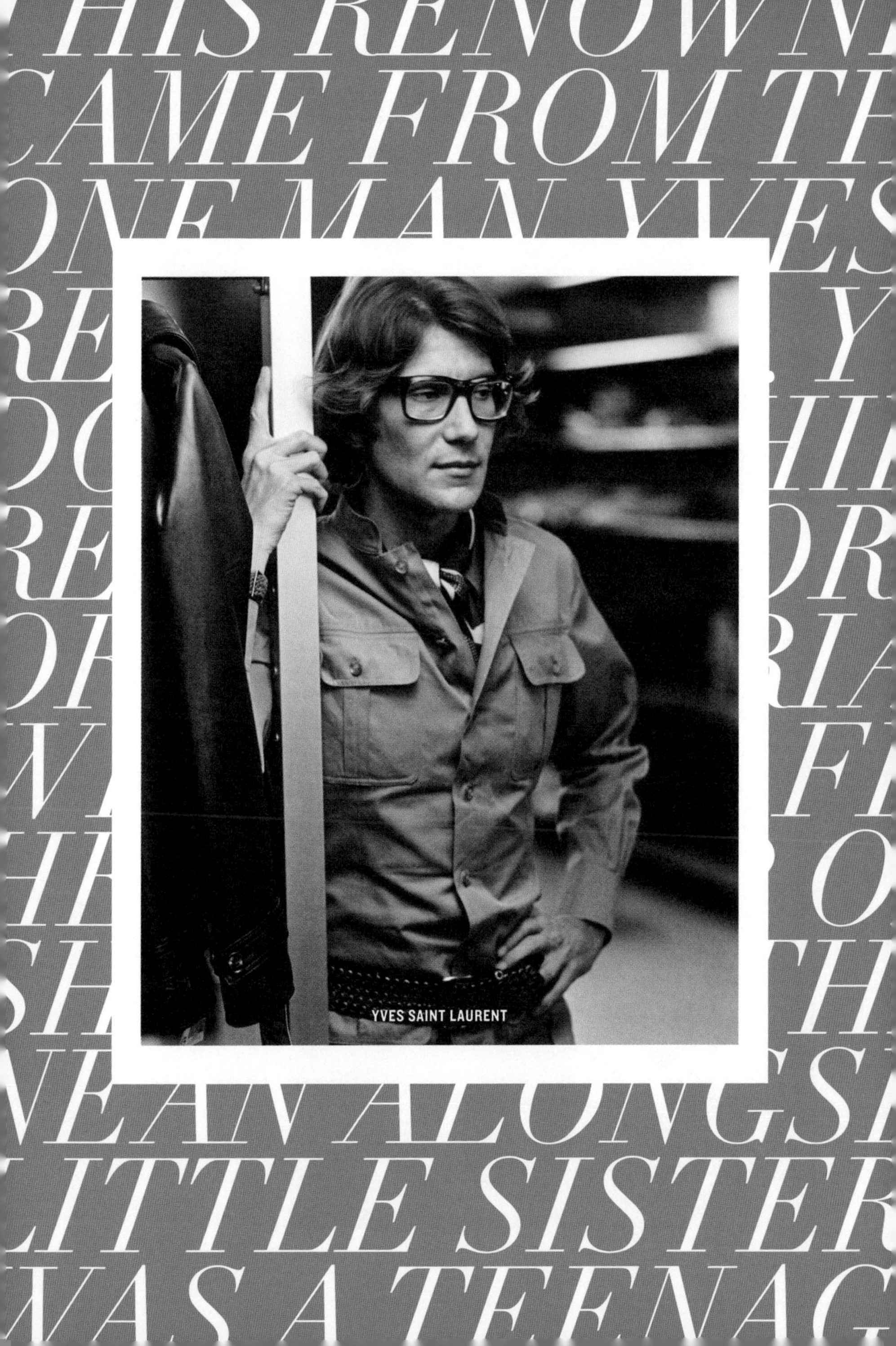
HIS RENOWN
CAME FROM TH
ONE MAN YVES
NEAN ALONGS
ITTLE SISTER
WAS A TEENAG
YVES SAINT LAURENT

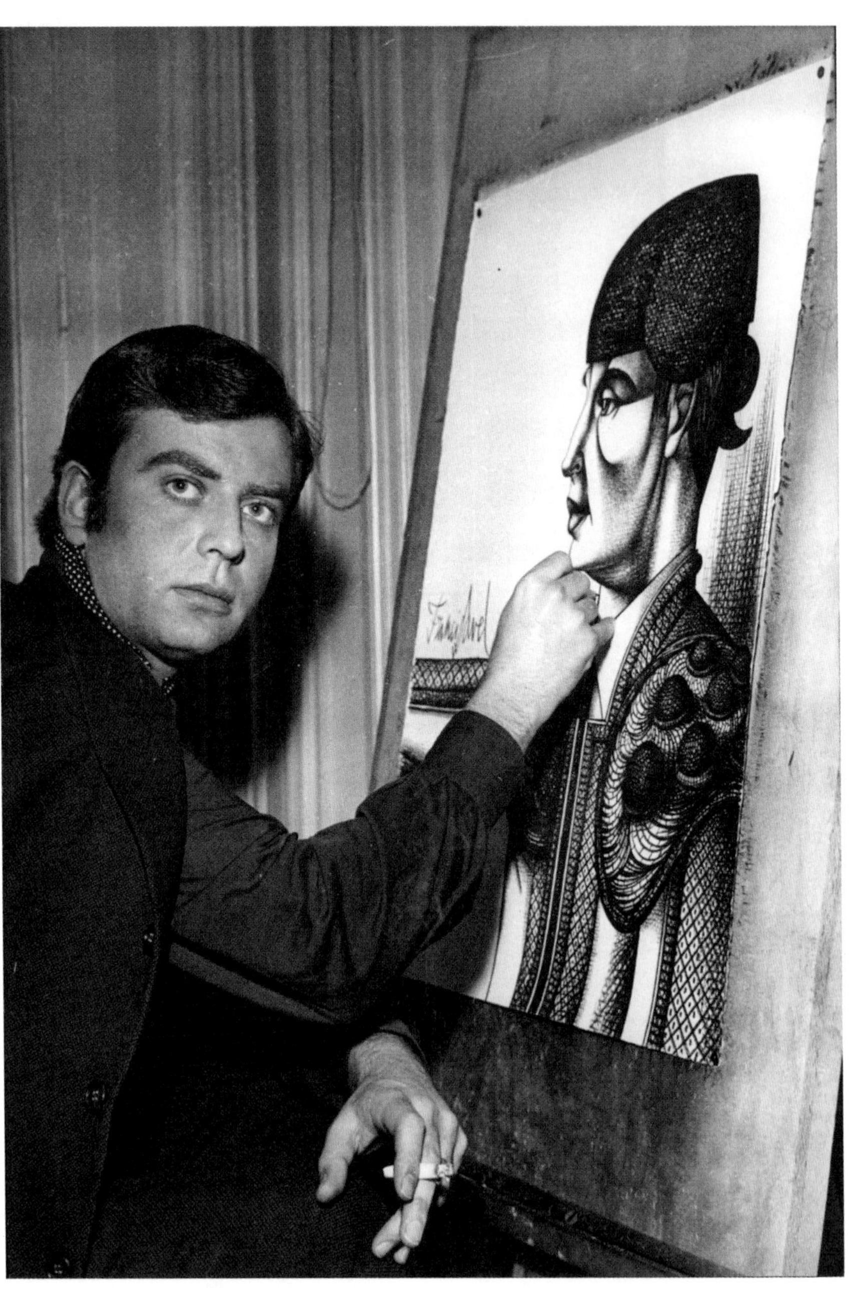

LIFELONG PARTNER
Pierre Bergé founded the fashion house with Yves Saint Laurent, named after the latter, in 1961, where they were not only business partners but also romantically involved. They separated on the personal front in 1976 but remained friends and business partners until their deaths.

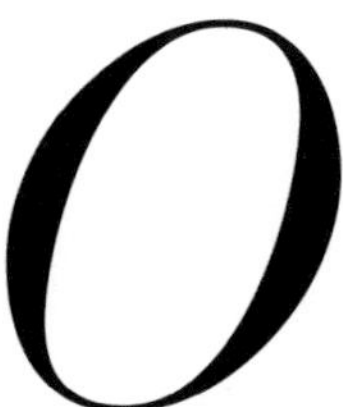

ne of the first major designs he did for Dior—Dovima with Elephants—was photographed by famed photographer Richard Avedon. The model wearing the dress was photographed alongside elephants from the French circus. The dress was gorgeous: sleek, black, with a sweetheart neckline and a giant white bow that swept down to the floor. This magical dress put Yves on the map. In 1957, he became Dior's head designer at the tender age of 21. Christian Dior passed away a few months later at the age of 52, so it was fortunate that he had discovered Yves' talent and trusted him to continue with his work for Dior, a fashion house that had only been around since 1946 but had become very popular and influential.

Yves continued to design for Dior for only a few more years. He parted ways with the company to start his own line after a contract dispute in 1960. He partnered with several other people in this new venture, including Pierre Berge and J. Mack Robinson. The first collection he produced for Yves Saint Laurent, or YSL, was the Spring 1962 collection. While people did not love this Spring collection, his Fall 1962 collection was met with rave reviews. Yves was on his way to becoming a hit in the fashion world.

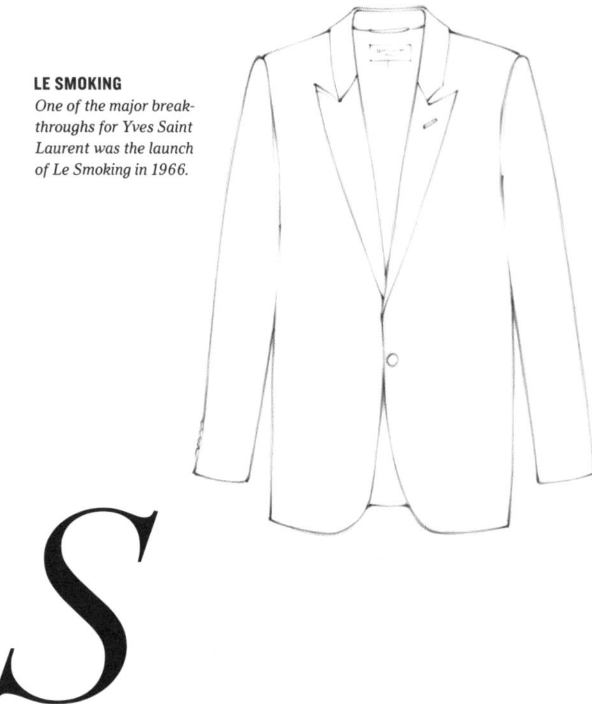

LE SMOKING
One of the major breakthroughs for Yves Saint Laurent was the launch of Le Smoking in 1966.

Since it was the 1960s, some of his looks catered to the beatnik counterculture movement. At this time, his famous designs included pea coats, thigh-high boots, safari jackets, and in 1966, Le Smoking, which was a tailored tuxedo jacket for women. The Le Smoking look was responsible for making it more acceptable for women to wear pants. He began to focus on ready-to-wear styles in addition to haute couture, which only made his collections more popular.

Hollywood started to take notice of his designs, especially actress Catherine Deneuve. Yves would go on to design costumes for many of her movies, including Love to Eternity and Mississippi Mermaid. The designer and the actress became quite close, embarking on a 50-year friendship that Catherine described as "my most beautiful love affair." At his fashion shows, she was always front and center in her support of Yves' work.

The '70s and '80s brought several popular styles: big shoulder pads, pumps, slim skirts, and regular-looking pantsuits. While some say that Yves was too focused on his social scene and partying at famous spots such as Studio 54 in New York City, he was still an important fixture in the fashion world, and in 1983, he was the first designer honored by the Metropolitan Museum of Art with a solo show featuring his work.

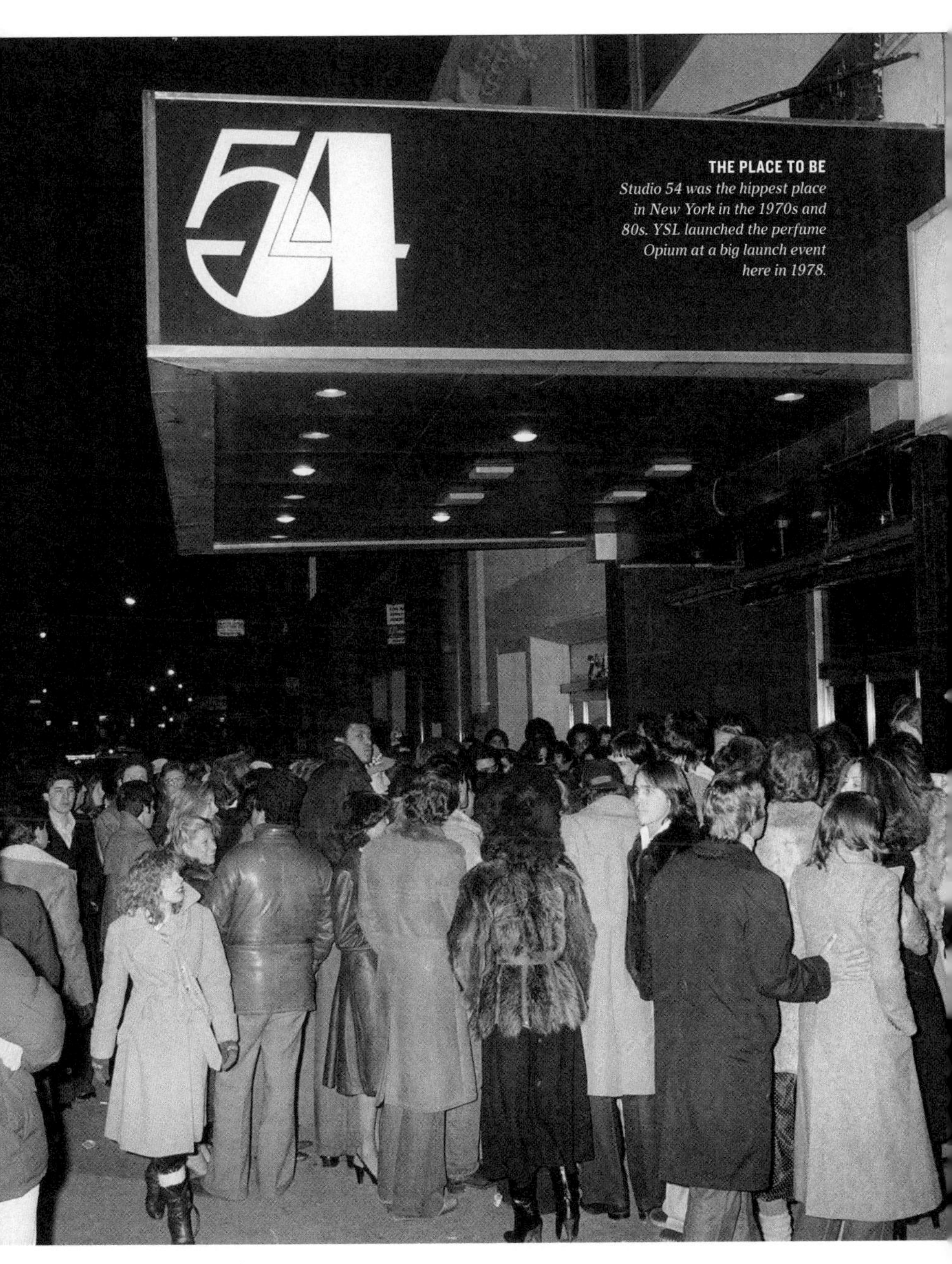

THE PLACE TO BE

Studio 54 was the hippest place in New York in the 1970s and 80s. YSL launched the perfume Opium at a big launch event here in 1978.

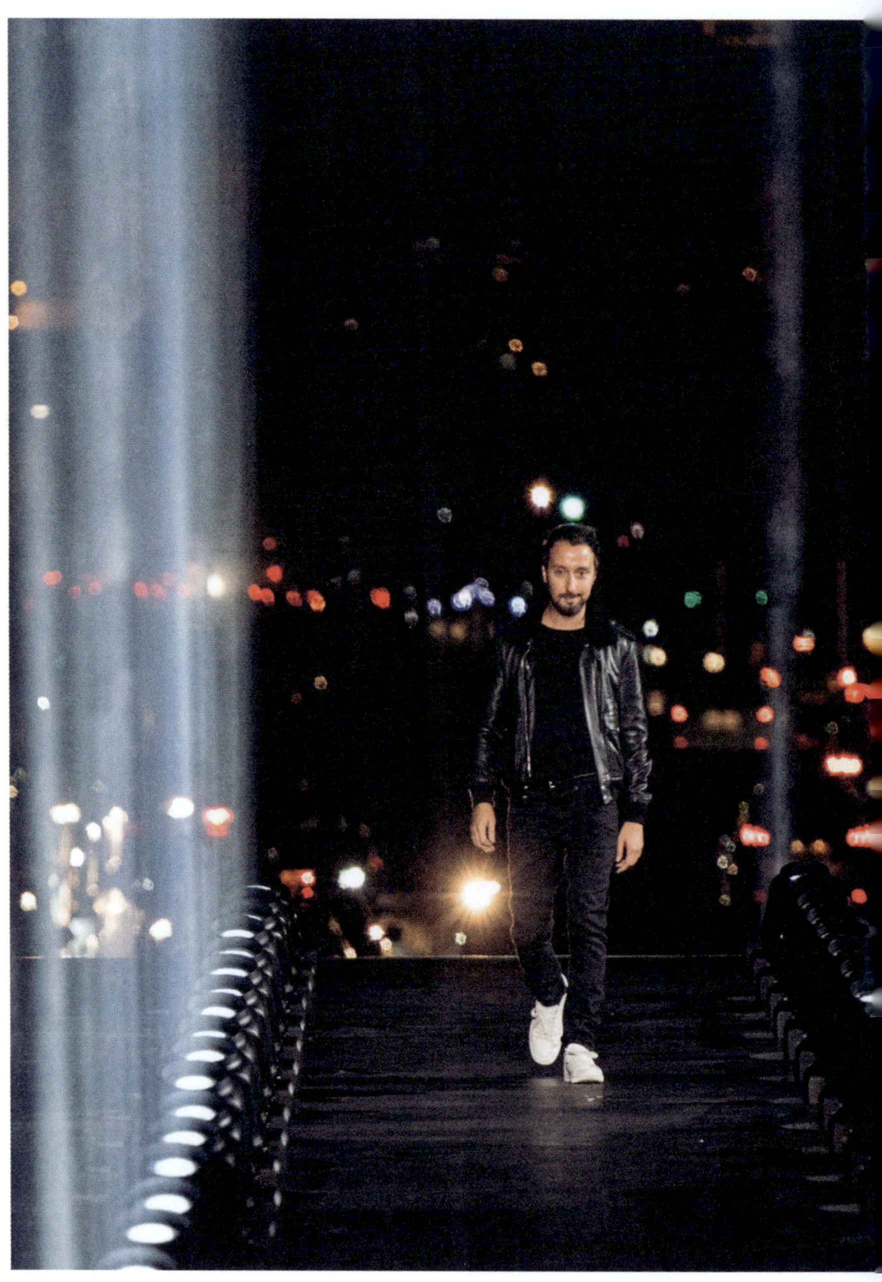

VACCARELLO
Since 2016, the Belgian-Italian designer Anthony Vaccarello has been at the helm of Yves Saint Laurent's designs with great success.

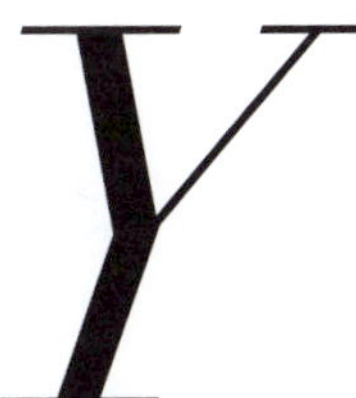

ves retired in 2002. While other designers, like Hedi Slimane and Tom Ford, were at the helm of creating for YSL, Yves continued to do some of the haute couture collections himself until he passed away from brain cancer at his apartment in Paris in 2008.

The work and legacy of Yves Saint Laurent is still alive and well in the company he created. YSL is now owned by Kering, a French global corporation that owns many luxury brands, including Gucci, Balenciaga, and Alexander McQueen, and purchased YSL in 1999. Since 2016, Anthony Vaccarello has been the creative director, or head designer, of the fashion house.

"I HAVE ALWAYS BELIEVED THAT FASHION WAS NOT ONLY TO MAKE WOMEN MORE BEAUTIFUL BUT ALSO TO REASSURE THEM, GIVE THEM CONFIDENCE."

Yves Saint Laurent

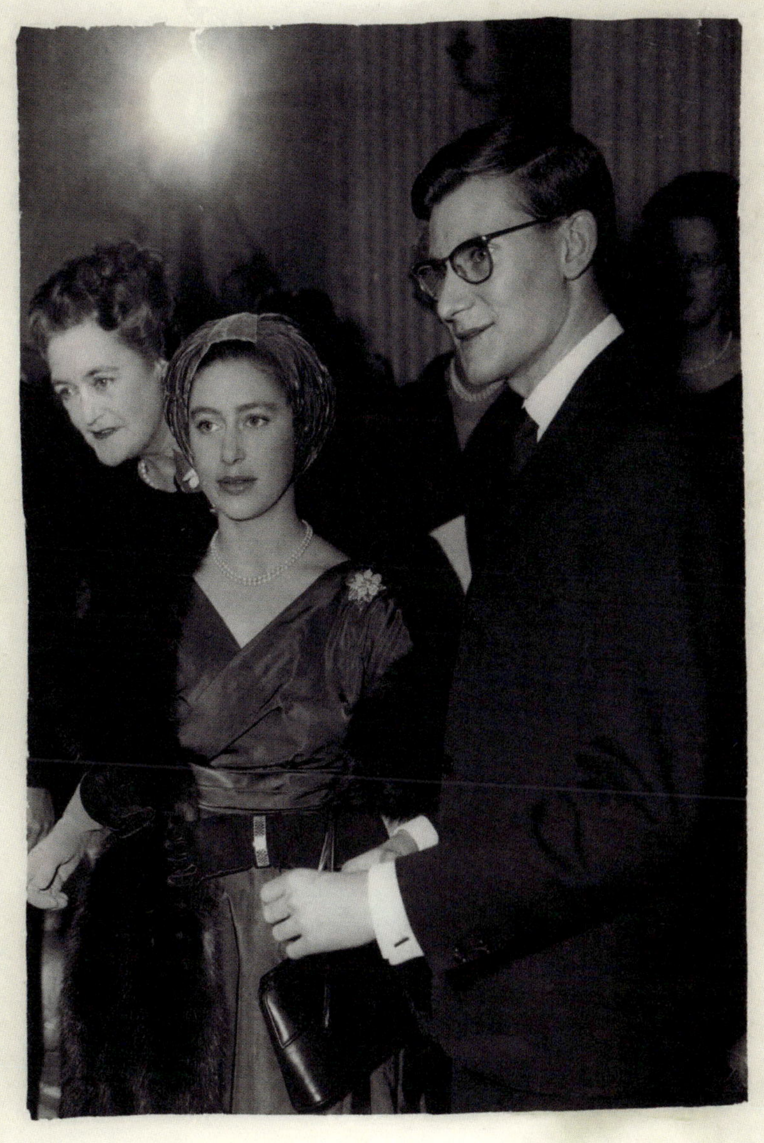

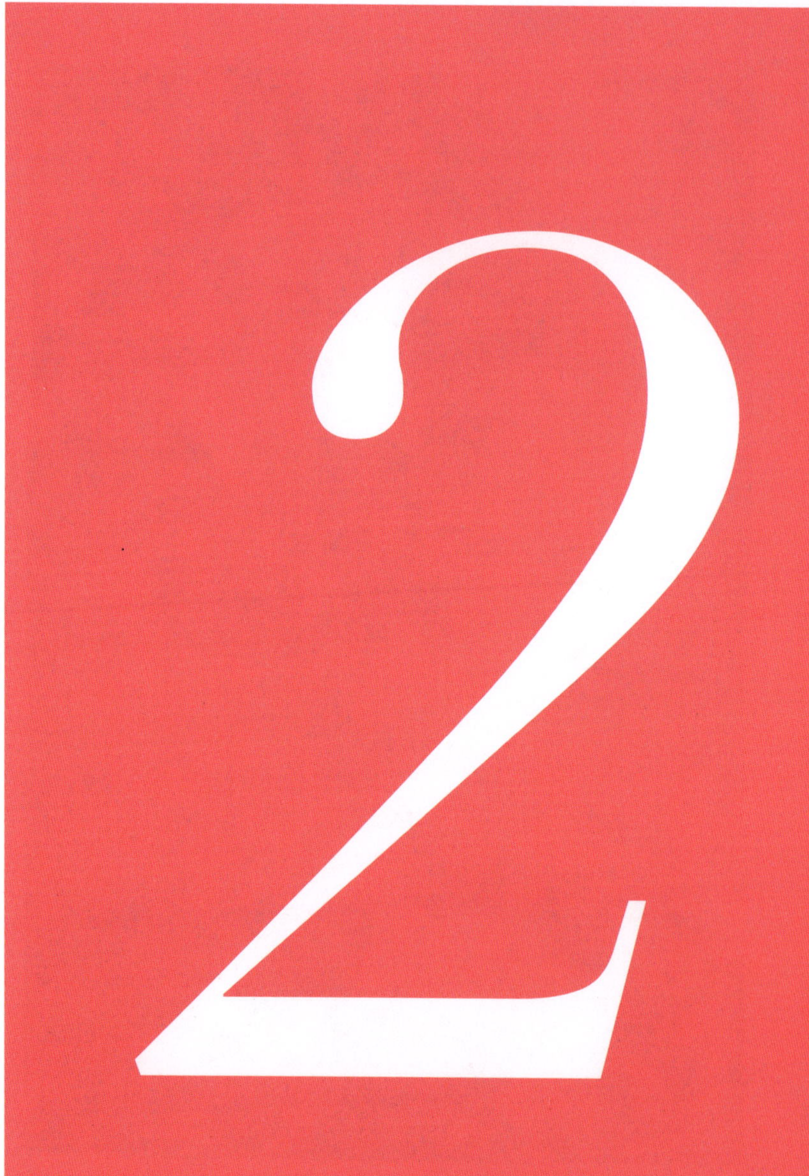

ALBER ELBAZ, TOM FORD, STEFANO PILATI, HEDI SLIMANE, *and* ANTHONY VACCARELLO

Notable Head Designers

OBVIOUSLY, YVES SAINT LAURENT designed for his own brand for many years. He created both haute couture and a ready-to-wear line, but once his health started to fail, the company hired assistants and other notable head designers.

The first was Alber Elbaz, who only managed to design three collections for the ready-to-wear Rive Gauche label. When Kering bought YSL in 1999, they fired Alber, even though he had been hired by Yves himself.

Alber's Fall 2000 look is considered the best of the three collections he produced for YSL. He managed to update the classic women's suit, making it timeless and chic. Each of the models on the runway wore long black gloves and matching leather ties. Some of the other looks were leather skirts with leather jackets and a full leather jumper. Most of the designs were black, in a variety of sleek and sexy styles.

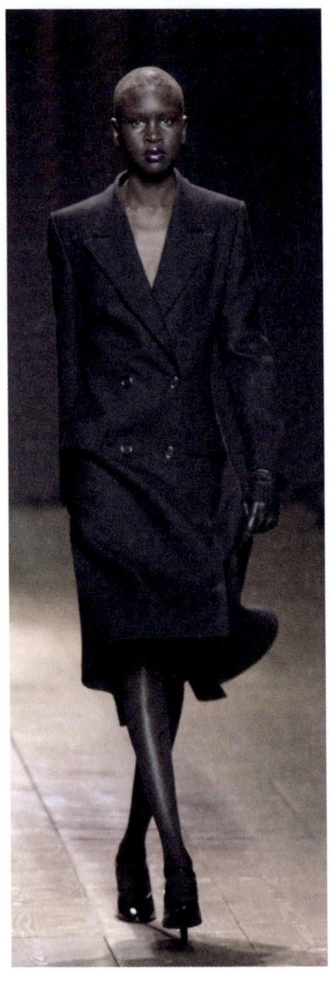

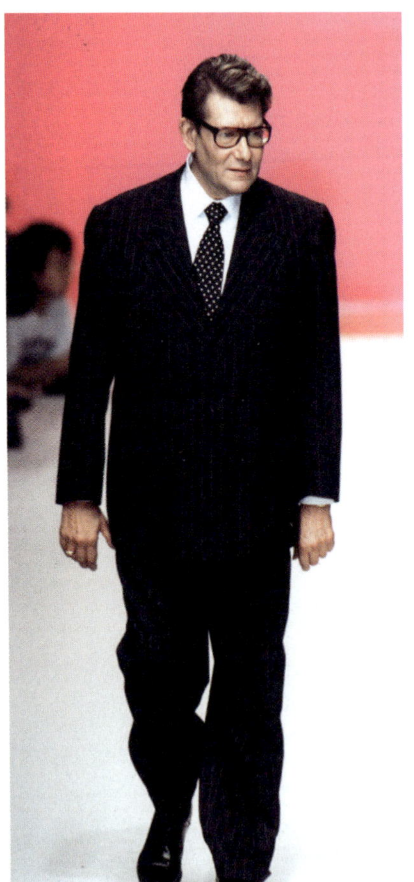

UPDATED CLASSICS
Albert Elbaz left his own mark on some of Yves Saint Laurent's classic designs, notably the iconic Le Smoking.

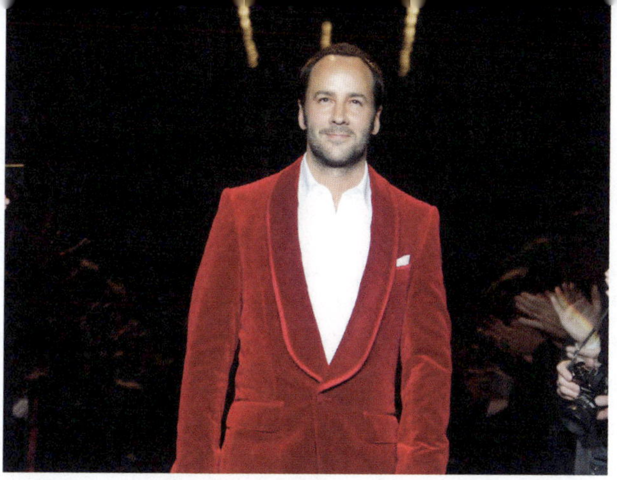

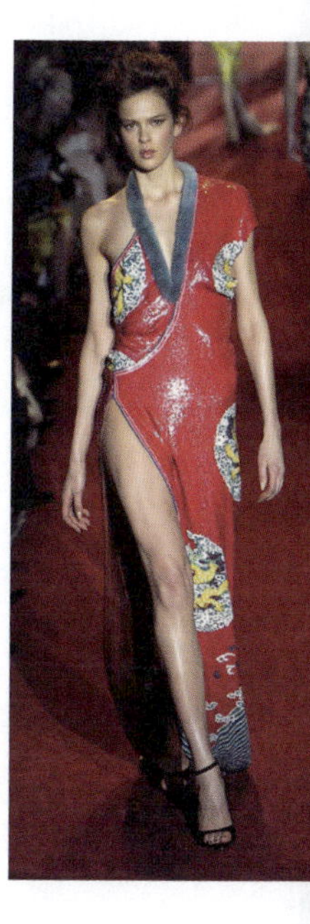

TOM *FORD*

The great Tom Ford was the next designer to take over YSL. He became the creative director of the entire fashion line, with the Spring 2001 collection being his first for the fashion house. Back then, Tom was still the creative director at Gucci, but with his phenomenal design skills, he created eight collections for YSL that were a big hit. Yves was still alive at the time, and it was said that he and Tom didn't get along very well. That is an understatement, since the feud between Tom and Yves was legendary in the fashion world.

For the first few years, they had been on good terms, with Tom overseeing at least 16 collections for YSL. With his success at Gucci, Tom was probably the biggest and most well-known designer in the world at the time. However, Yves and Tom no longer got along once Yves thought that Tom was changing too much of YSL's core look with his own ideas. In a famous message to Tom, Yves said, "In 13 minutes on the runway, you have destroyed 40 years of my career." Clearly, Yves was not happy with Tom, even though his designs had been selling quite well for YSL. Tom left the fashion house in 2004.

Some of Tom's most notable designs for YSL were the last he did for the label. He finally caved to Yves' wishes and incorporated the famed Le Smoking jacket into the collection for 2003, but he did it in silk and white. Tom's final collection for 2004 was a drastic departure from the classic YSL look; he figured that if he was on his way out, he was going to do exactly as he pleased with the line. The 2004 collection was Asia-inspired, with jewel tones, fur touches, and whimsical buttons that had pictures of frogs on them, oddly enough. Tom even wore a version of the Le Smoking jacket in bright red, which Yves probably hated.

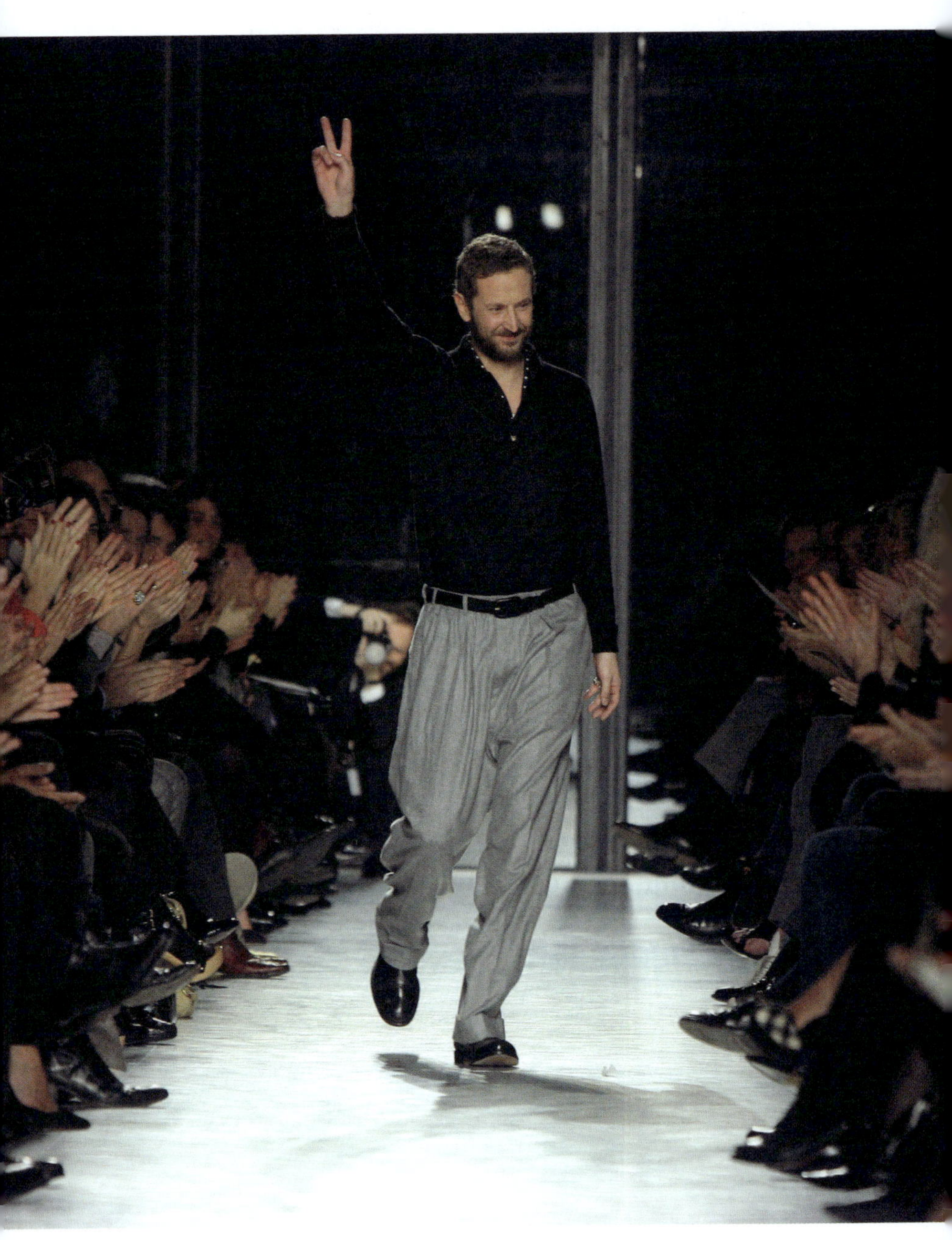

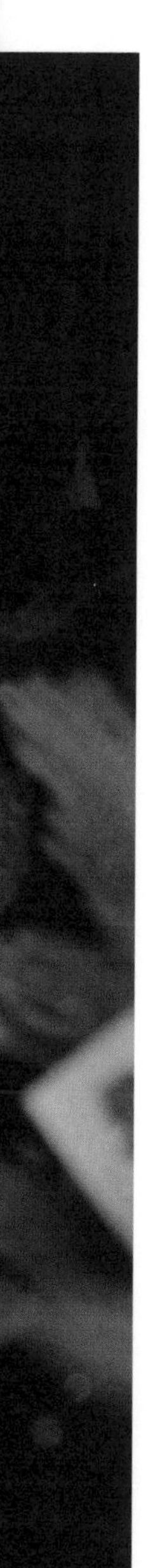

STEFANO *PILATI*

Next up as creative director of YSL was Stefano Pilati, an Italian designer. He was already working for the company, since Tom Ford had hired him in 2000 for the women's ready-to-wear line. The promotion allowed him the freedom to design for both YSL's men's and women's lines. Yves was extremely critical of Stefano's work during his time there, but that was probably just due to the fact that Yves wasn't going to truly love anyone's work other than his own.

This was a tough time for YSL. Many of Stefano's collections were celebrated while others were not. The company was experiencing financial hardship at the time and had to close several stores around the world, including those in San Francisco, New York, and Chicago. The New York closure was especially sad, since the Madison Avenue location was the first to open in the United States when YSL came over from Paris. Stefano managed to hang on to the position of creative director for eight years. For his first collection, he wanted to do something completely different than Tom had done during his time at YSL. Thus, the Spring 2005 collection was very girly, with tons of ruffles and bows. One of the key pieces was a tulip skirt, which was very popular. The entire collection was a departure from what YSL and Tom had designed previously, and many people in the fashion world absolutely hated it. In the eight years that Stefano designed for YSL, he managed to create more successful collections than failures, but it was a very up-and-down ride.

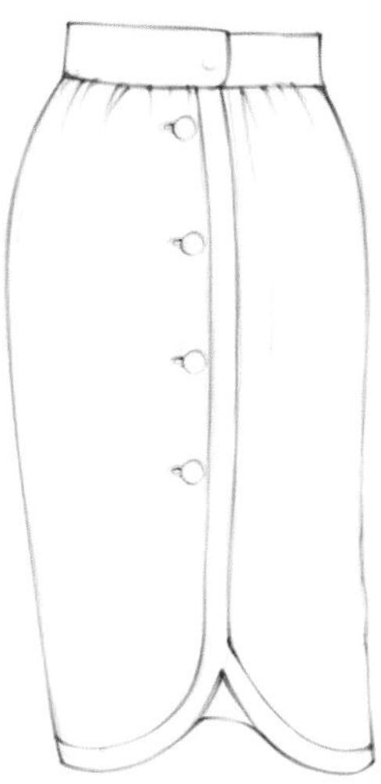

TULIP SKIRT
Under the creative direction of Stefano Pilati, the Tulip Skirt retained its iconic silhouette while incorporating modern elements.

HEDI *SLIMANE*

Hedi Slimane was brought in by Kering to replace Stefano in 2012. Even though YSL hadn't produced haute couture in a few years, Hedi brought it back. He was responsible for dropping the "Yves" from Yves Saint Laurent, with the brand coming to be known as just Saint Laurent or YSL. This caused a major shock in the fashion industry; it was a controversial move and one that many people in the industry thought was disrespectful to the memory of Yves Saint Laurent.

Some of his best looks for the brand were those in the Spring 2013 collection, where he revamped the famous YSL 1967 Safari Jacket, giving it a rock n' roll edge and makeover. He cinched the waist, made it in sleek black leather, and secured it with a bunch of thin straps. Stefano stayed with YSL until 2016, when he parted ways with the company on good terms.

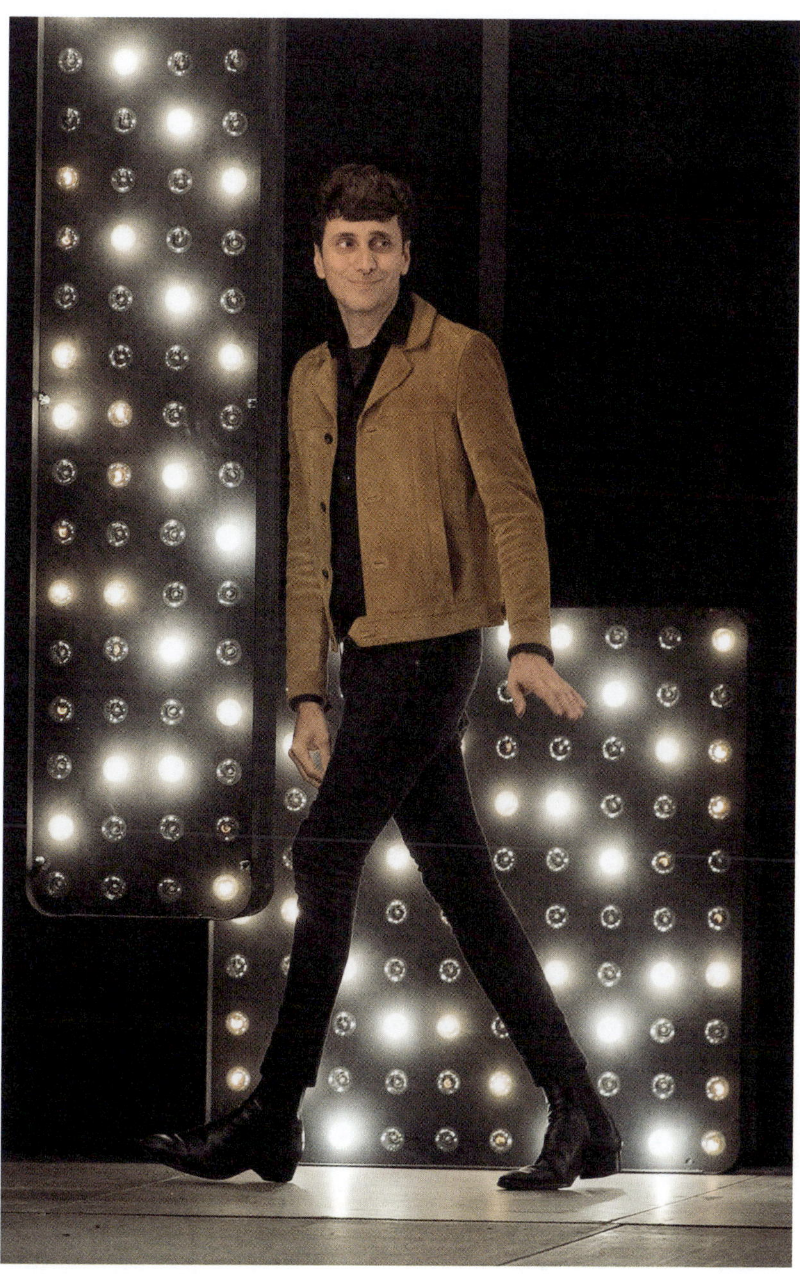

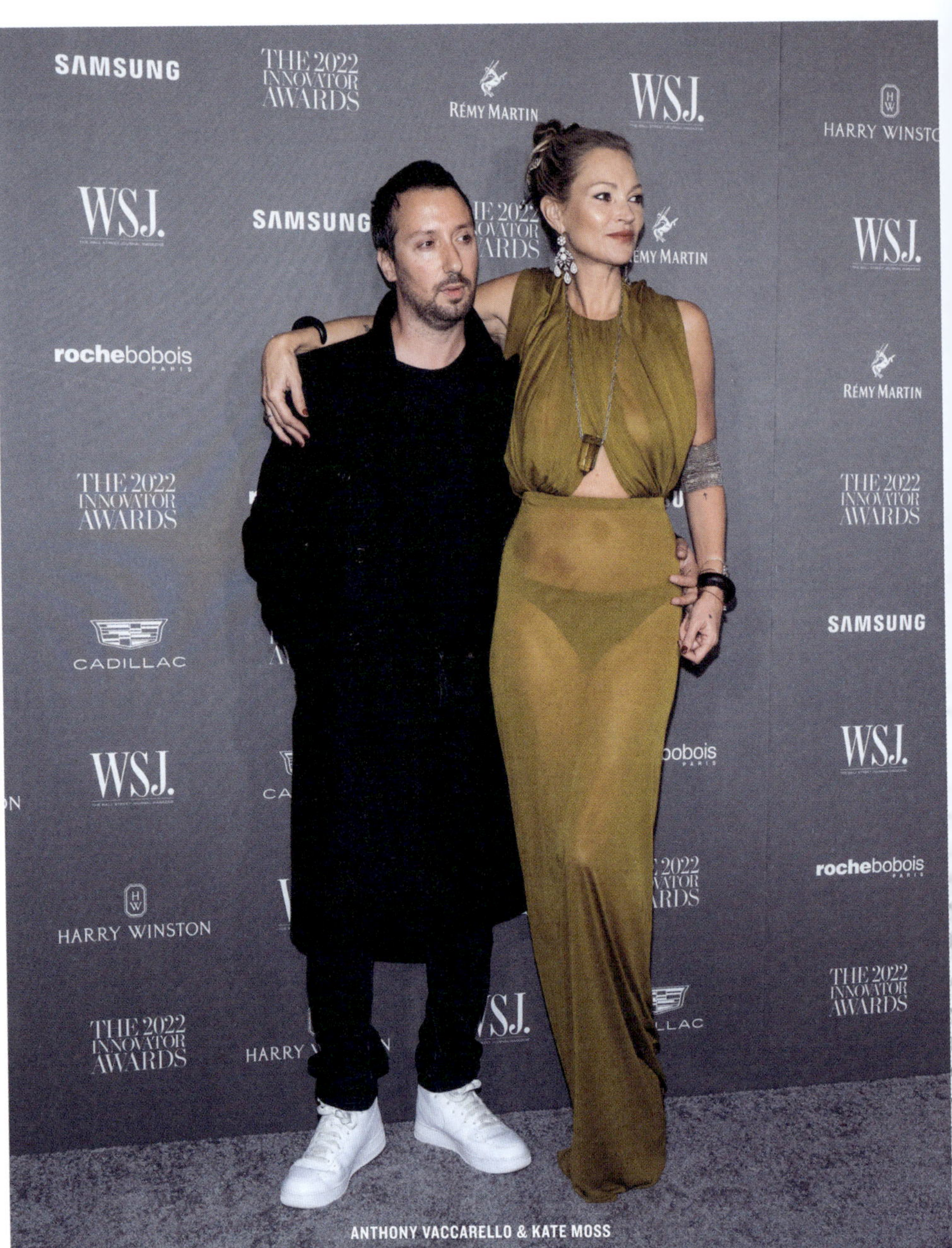

ANTHONY VACCARELLO & KATE MOSS

ANTHONY *VACCARELLO*

The current creative director of YSL is Anthony Vaccarello, a Belgian-Italian fashion designer. Since his first year in 2016, he has been a huge boost for the company, with sales having increased by 25 percent. His background as a fashion designer includes working under Karl Lagerfeld for Fendi for two years, and he worked as creative director at Versace for a short time. Donatella Versace absolutely loved him.

When he was hired by YSL, he was 34 years old and relatively unknown. Over the eight years he has been at the company, his work for YSL has been applauded by the industry. He has managed to make YSL his own, even under heavy scrutiny from the ghost of Yves Saint Laurent. Yves is credited with creating the modern women's style. Trying to keep new ideas in the mix while adhering to what the House of YSL stands for is a big task, and luckily Anthony has been up to the challenge. Many people say he's the best designer YSL has ever had.

Some of his designs to date have combined edgy silhouettes with pops of color and interesting patterns. Texture is a vital part of his collections, with silks meshing with leather and chiffon in cool ways. It's fun to imagine what his next collections will bring, and fashionistas always look forward to the next YSL statement-making looks.

"CHANEL GAVE WOMEN FREEDOM. YVES SAINT LAURENT GAVE THEM POWER."

Pierre Bergé

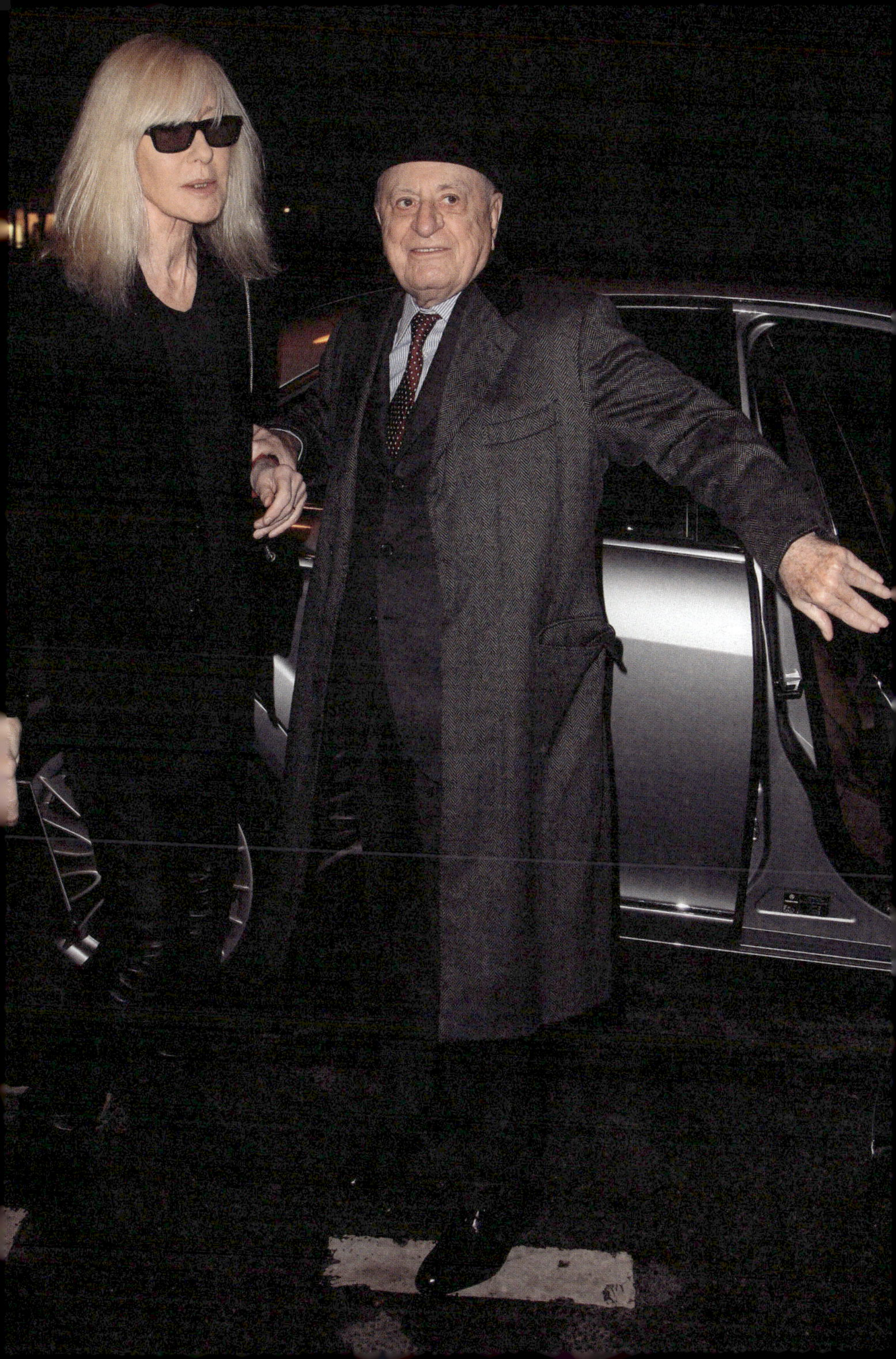

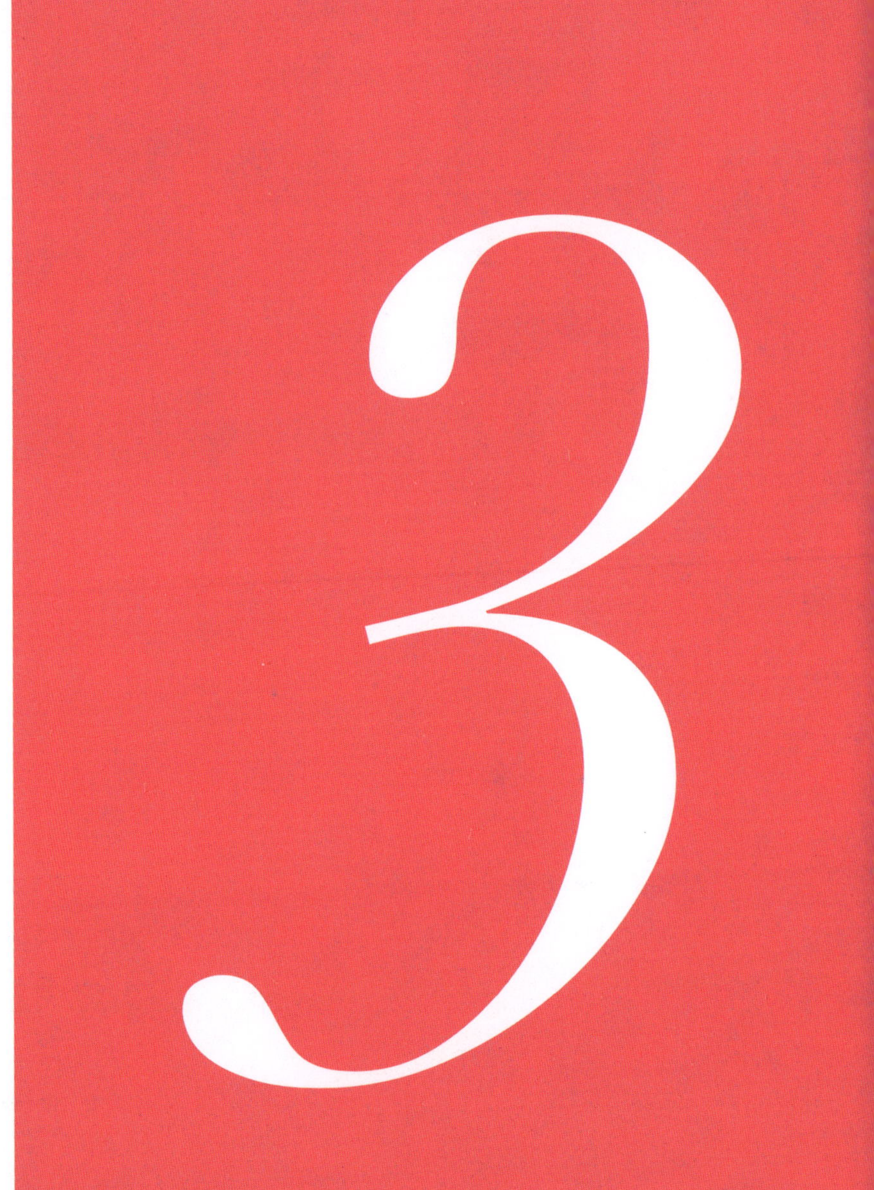
3

TIMES WHERE YSL MADE *the HEADLINES*

In the News

SOMETIMES A FASHION HOUSE MAKES THE NEWS solely because of its designs, while at other times, it's due to scandals. From tax evasion to oddball designs, Yves Saint Laurent—the man and the company—has been the focus of eye-catching headlines. Yves himself made plenty of headlines for taking part in the worldwide party scene of the 1970s and '80s. Let's look at some of the most shocking news stories involving YSL through the decades, starting with Yves and Studio 54.

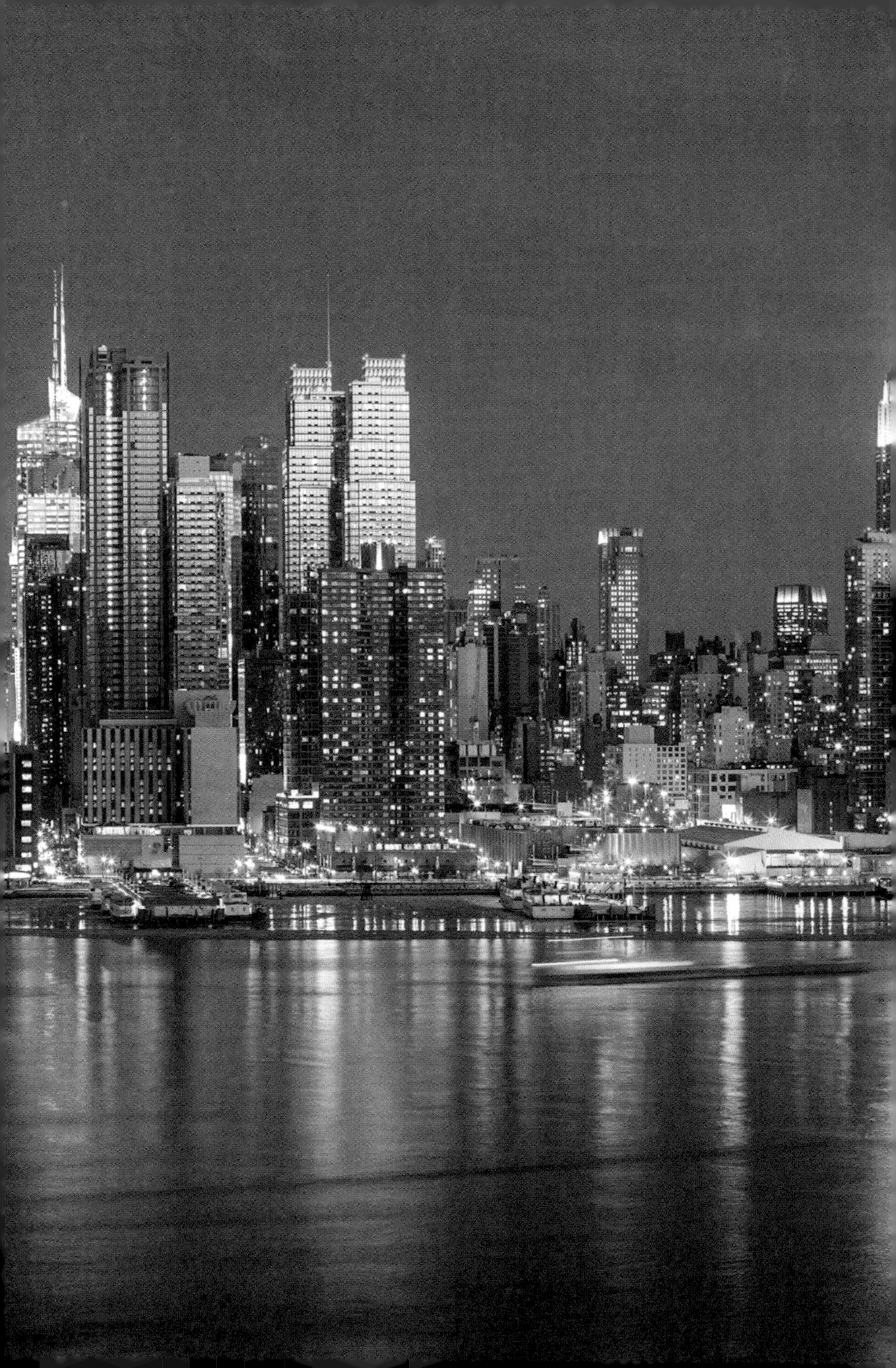

YVES SAINT LAURENT'S

PARTY DAYS

Yves was a big part of the Manhattan and worldwide high-society party scene in the 1970s and '80s. He was a regular fixture at Studio 54 in New York, a disco-like nightclub that was popular with glitterati celebrities such as Bianca Jagger, David Bowie, and Truman Capote. Yves was regularly photographed out on the town with his various friends, making headlines that were less than favorable. The owner of Studio 54, Steve Rubell, was more than happy to cater to whatever Yves needed, as he did for all his well-known friends. In 1978, Yves even launched the first fragrance for YSL, Opium, at Studio 54.

This period involved a lot of illegal drugs and alcohol for the famed designer. It was well-known that Yves had a dark side. Tom Ford, who designed for YSL for quite a few years and was close to Yves, said that he could be "so difficult, and so evil." Yet, by the 1990s, Yves was doing much better, replacing his alcohol consumption with a daily habit of multiple cans of soda.

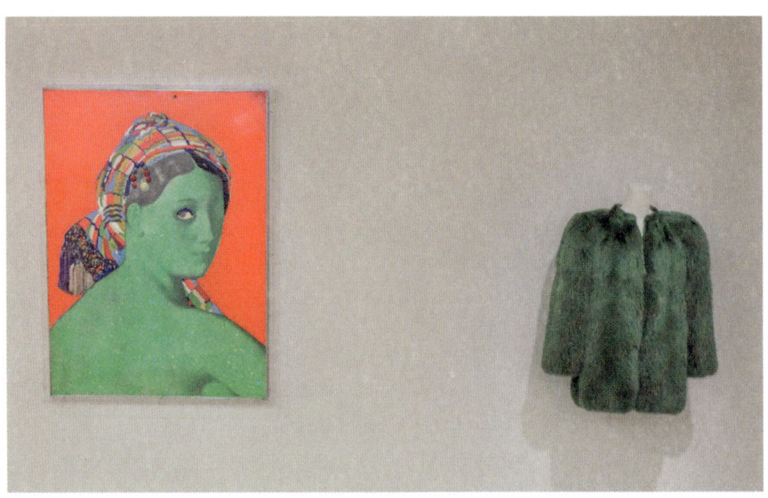

YVES SAINT LAURENT'S *1971* COLLECTION

Yves Saint Laurent's 1971 collection, also known as the Forties or Liberation Collection, came out in January of 1971 and was a tribute to the wartime fashion of the 1940s. It was a very odd coupling. Yves was inspired by Paloma Picasso, a high society friend and the youngest daughter of artist Pablo Picasso. The reason the collection was so scandalous is because it celebrated the Nazi German occupation of France during the war. It was characterized by knee-length dresses with fur accents and wedge shoes. When they premiered it on the runway, the models wore garish makeup, which was a popular look at the time.

Some fashion critics loved it, while others hated it and referred to the collection as the "Scandal Collection." The dark memories of those war days still haunted many people in the '70s, as they still do today, so this collection clearly was not Yves' best move. Some headlines called it the "Ugliest Collection in Paris."

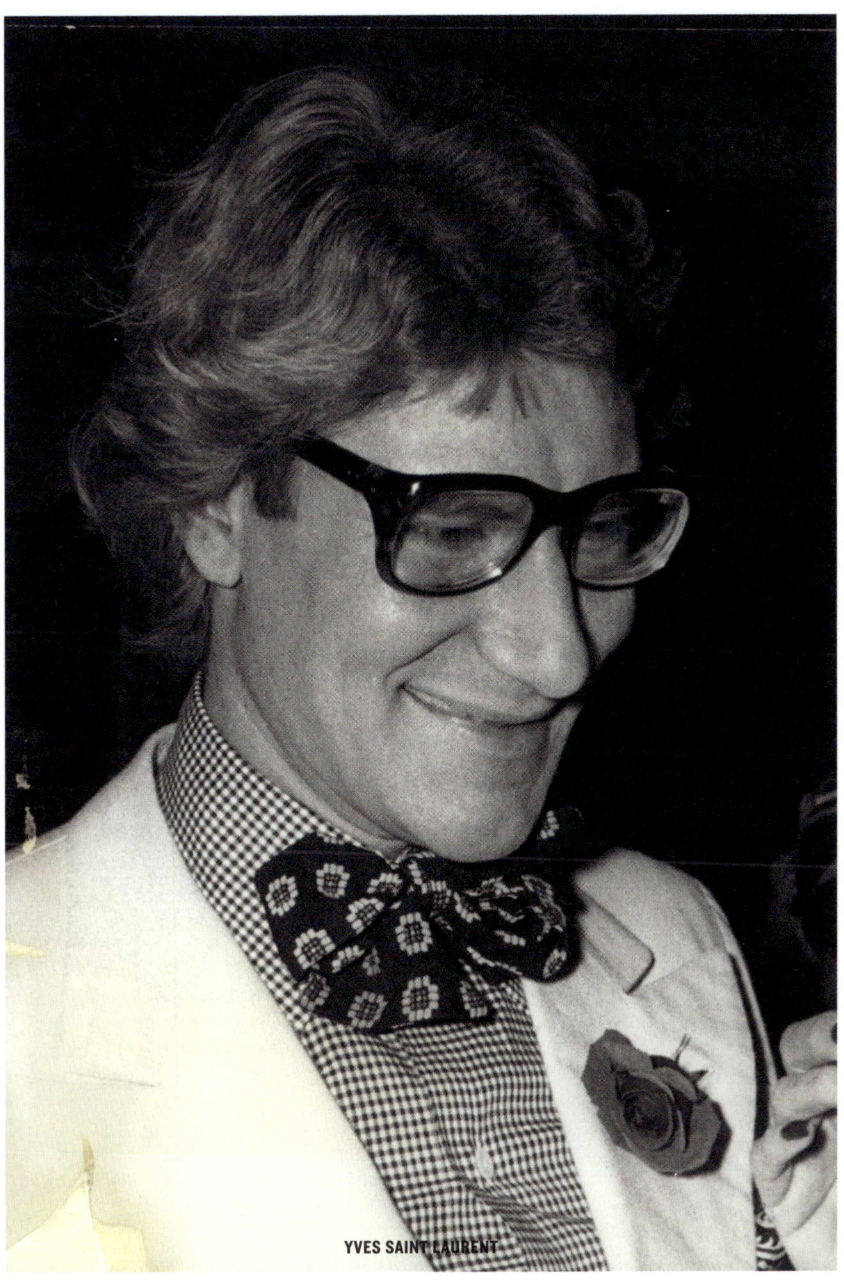

YVES SAINT LAURENT

A PARIS BOUTIQUE UPSETS YSL

Colette, a popular boutique in Paris, came up with what YSL considered an unpopular t-shirt design: black t-shirts that simply said, "Ain't Laurent Without Yves." These shirts were produced in response to Hedi Slimane being made the new creative director of Yves Saint Laurent. Hedi wanted to revive the haute couture line and moved the design studio to Los Angeles, California, which many people thought took away from the French heritage of the brand. Hedi was also the one who dropped Yves from Yves Saint Laurent to change the name of the company to Saint Laurent. It was in response to all these events that the infamous t-shirts were created. YSL had done business with Colette for years, but when these t-shirts came out, that immediately stopped.

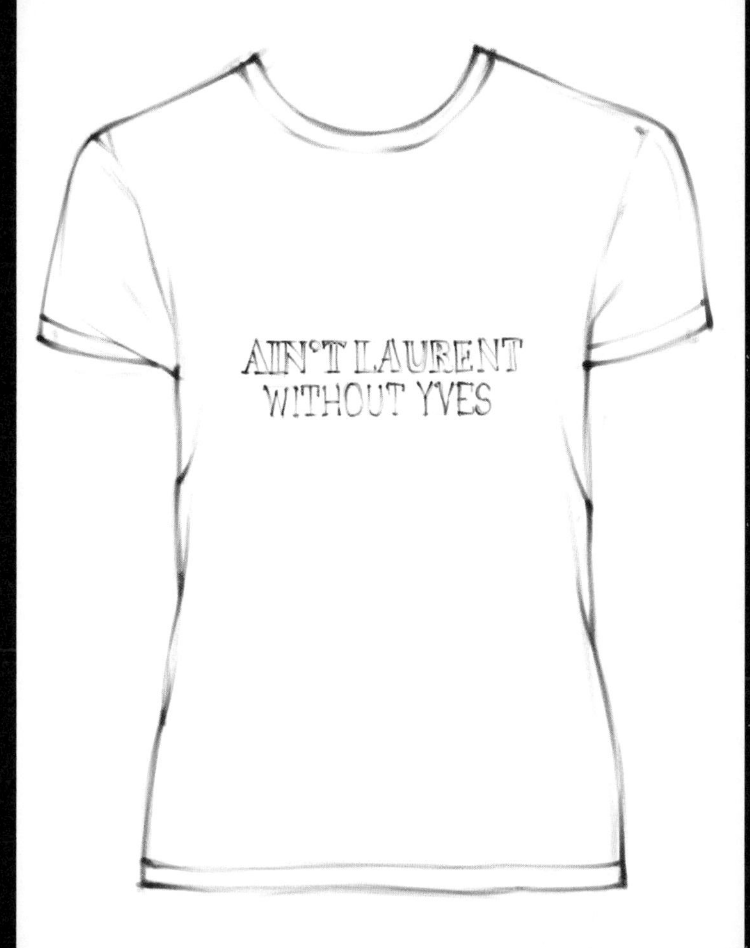
AIN'T LAURENT
WITHOUT YVES

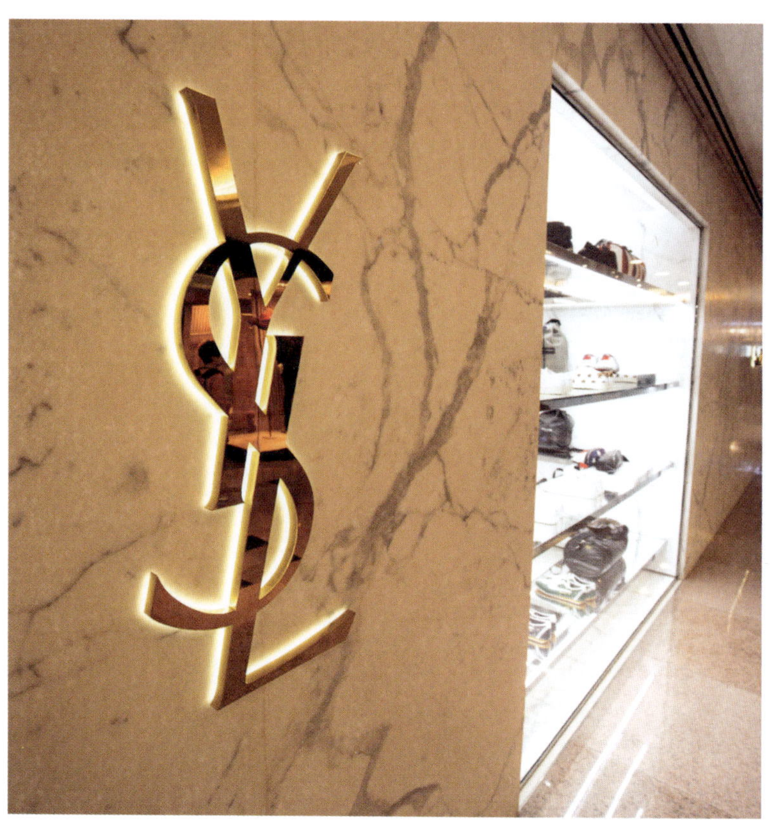

BIG-TIME YSL TAX EVASION

Between 2009 and 2017, Kering, the parent company of Yves Saint Laurent, was accused of evading taxes in France, to the tune of $180 million, after declaring its profits in Switzerland, which has a much lower tax rate than France. Other companies that Kering owned also saved money this way, including Gucci and Balenciaga.

Finally, in 2022, Kering resolved the matter, and France closed the case. It is estimated that the company settled with the French government for approximately $210 million. Kering didn't even bother to comment on the matter when it was finalized, with someone in the company's PR department simply calling it "old news."

HEDI SLIMANE SUES YSL AND WINS

In 2018, Hedi Slimane, one of the former creative directors of the brand, sued YSL and won. The lawsuit claimed that Kering had underpaid him during his tenure with the fashion house. He was awarded around $8 million. It is estimated that during Hedi's four years with the brand, sales tripled, but in his final year, he was only paid around $700,000. There was a clause in his contract that stipulated that YSL would pay him at least $10 million per year. It wasn't great for Kering, a luxury conglomerate worth at least $41 billion, to be seen to be treating one of their top designers that way.

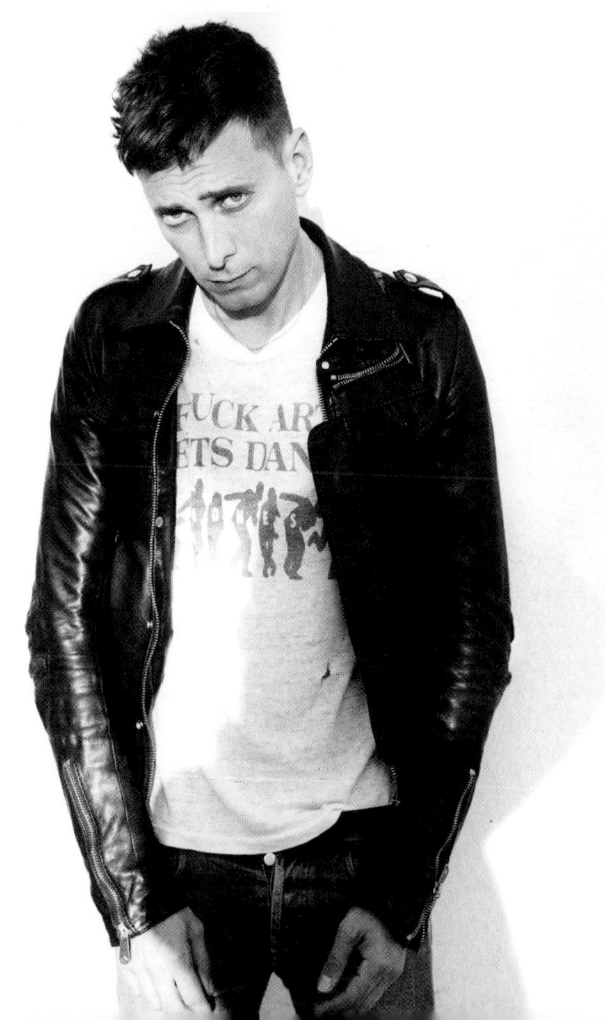

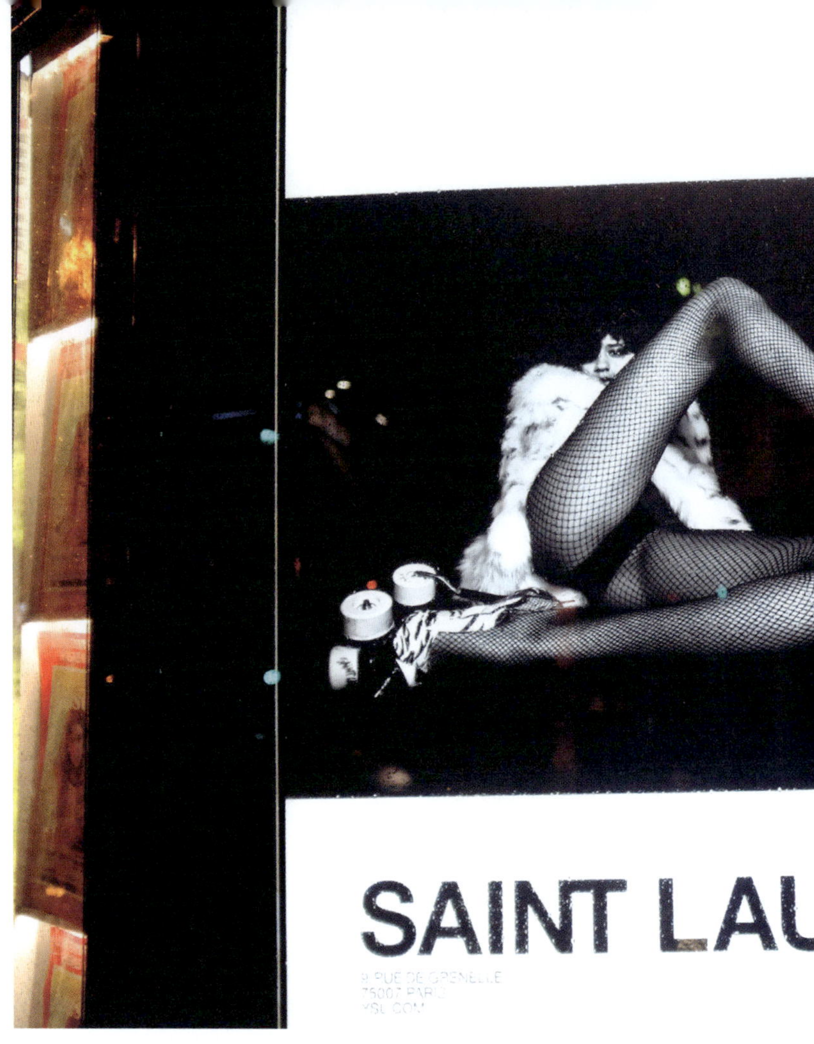

FALL 2017

SUPER SKINNY MODELS

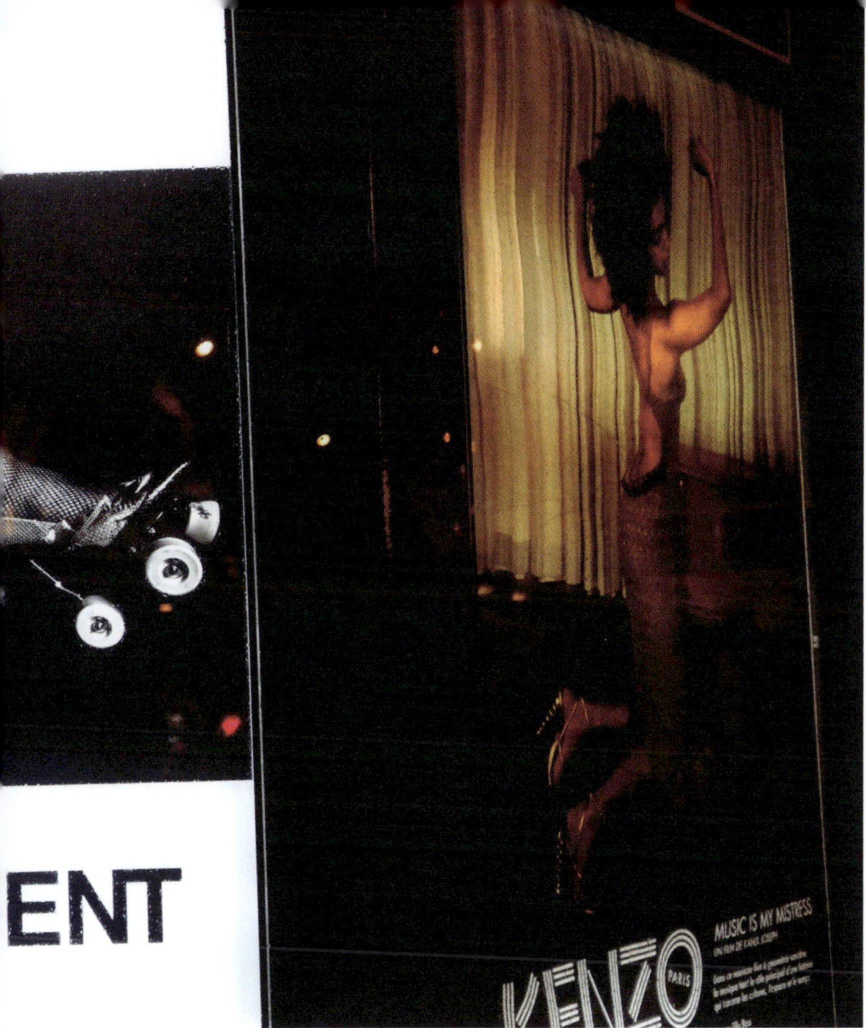

Models are notoriously skinny, especially the ones that walk the runway and model haute couture. But Yves Saint Laurent went a little too far with the Fall 2017 campaign. In the British Elle Magazine, the company's ad showed a model who looked to be unhealthy and anorexic. The British regulatory department responsible for advertising banned it almost immediately.

French advertising standards made YSL remove two poster-style ads that featured the models. Not only were the models too thin, but they were in what was considered degrading poses. Fernanda Oliveira was one of the models in those ads. Wearing fishnets, a leotard, and roller skates, she was seated on the ground with her legs splayed open. The images were taken for Anthony Vaccarello's debut collection for the fashion house.

“YVES SAINT LAURENT WAS NOT JUST A FASHION DESIGNER; *HE WAS A CULTURAL ICON.*”

Tom Ford

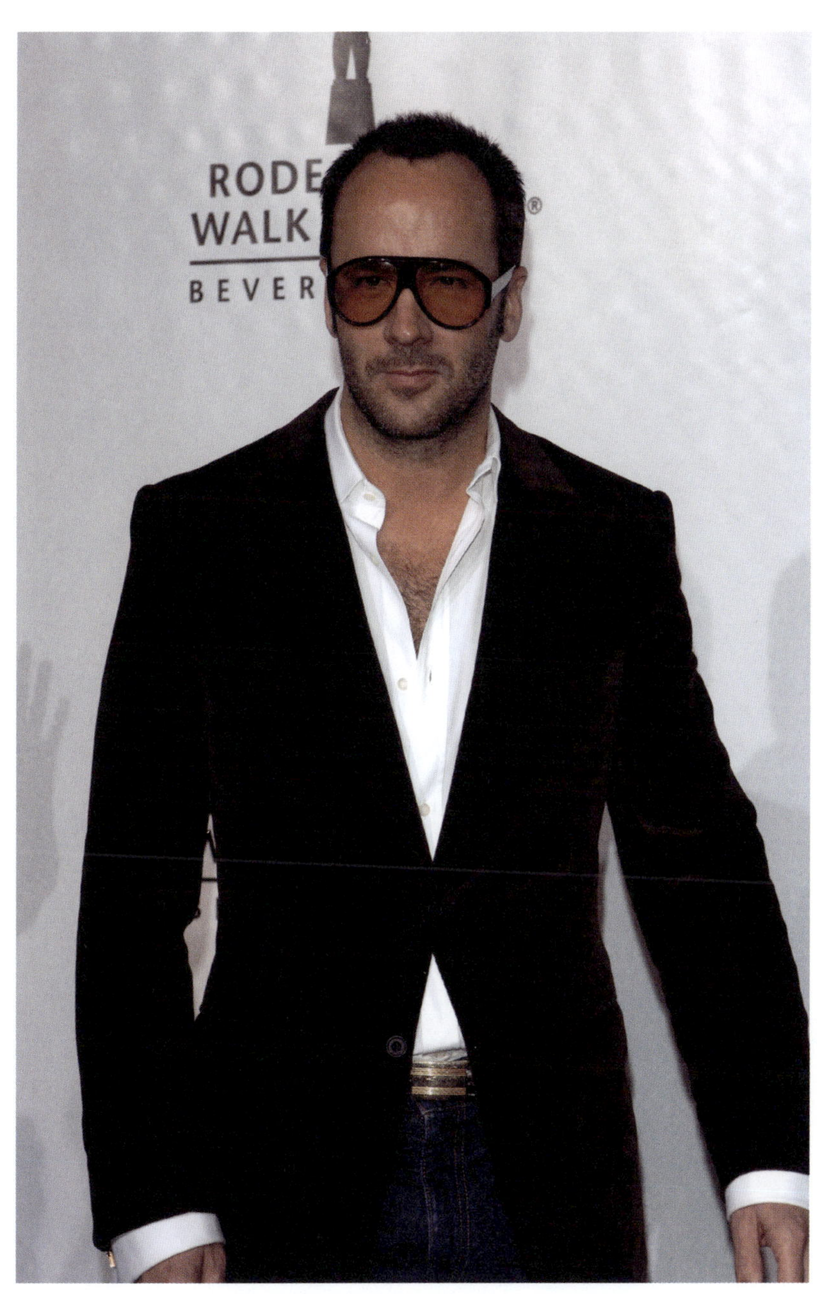
RODE
WALK
BEVER

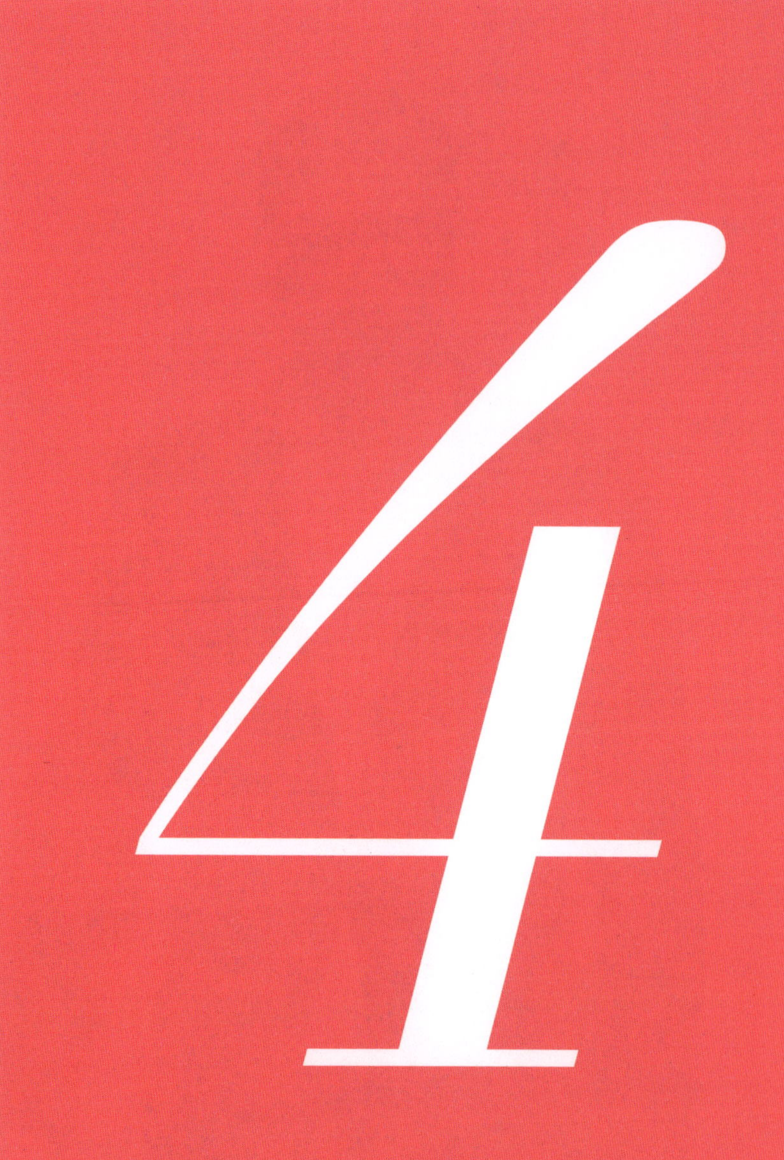

YSL'S LE SMOKING TUXEDO JACKET *and* BEYOND

Clothing

JUST FIVE YEARS AFTER Yves Saint Laurent launched his clothing line in 1966, the defining piece of clothing was created. It was called Le Smoking and was part of his Pop Art Collection. In French, the name means "tuxedo," and that's exactly what Le Smoking was—a tuxedo-style jacket for women. This style of jacket was inspired by the traditional men's jacket, but the tailoring made it different. The collar was sleeker, and the jacket nipped in at the waist to give a woman more shape compared to the boxy look of a men's jacket.

Yves once said of the suit: "A woman wearing a suit is anything but masculine. It accentuates her femininity, her seductiveness, her ambiguity." There is some debate over where exactly Yves found the inspiration to create this style of jacket. It may have been from the famed actress Marlene Dietrich, who was known for wearing men's style clothing in the '40s and '50s. It was a fashion-forward and slightly scandalous look that she loved. Some trace it back to Yves' model muse, Danielle Luquet de Saint German, who was well-known for her fluid, androgynous style. As a longtime friend and muse of Yves, Danielle had more than 300 pieces of YSL couture, which were auctioned off in 2013 as part of a 10,000-piece collection of clothing from different luxury design houses. When they met in the 1960s, Danielle became a sort of "It Girl" under the direction of Yves, who thought her style was fabulous.

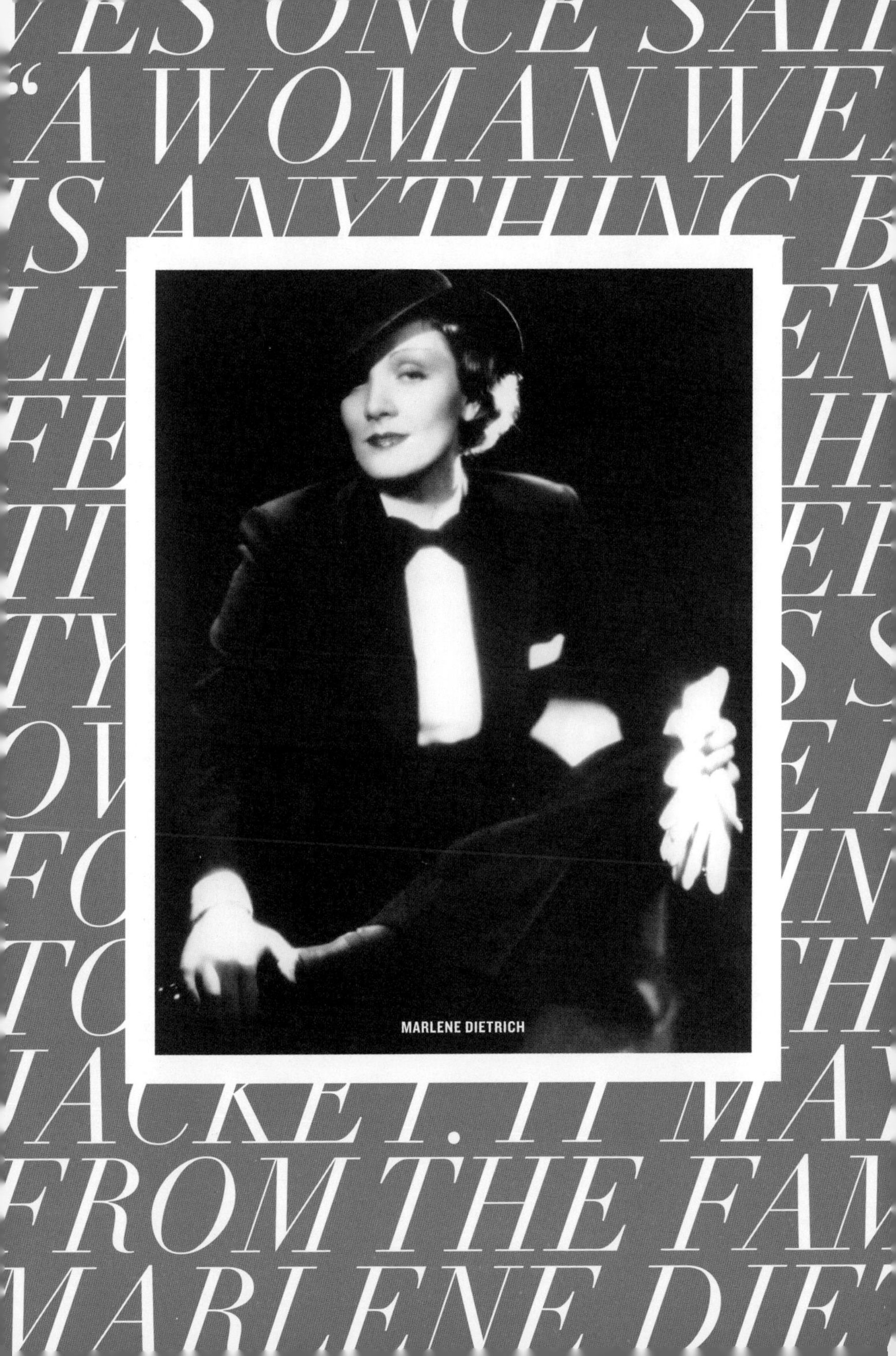

MARLENE DIETRICH

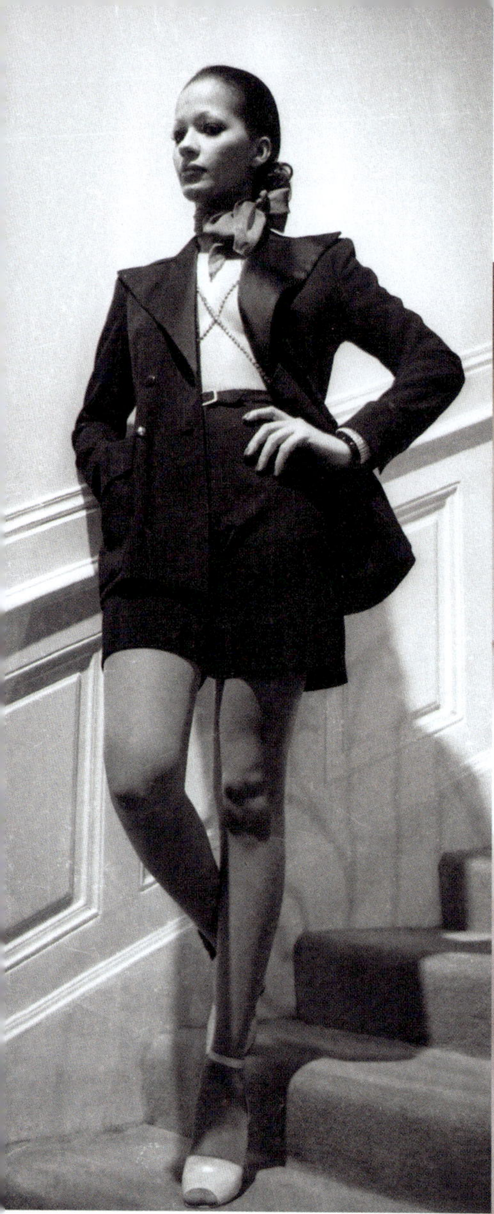

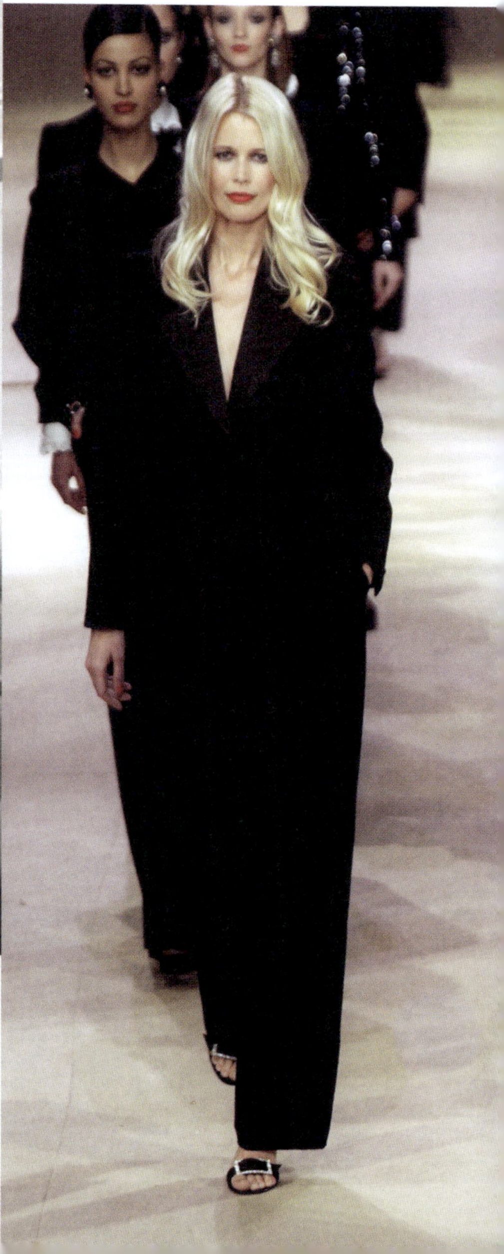

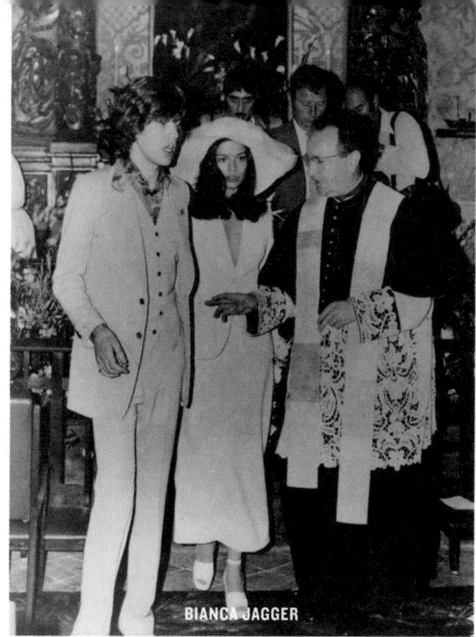
BIANCA JAGGER

LE SMOKING

The look of Le Smoking paired with pants was obviously a departure from what most women would wear to go out or attend an event at that time. That's what makes Yves' vision so extraordinary and revolutionary for couture women's clothing. He even introduced Le Smoking to the Rive Gauche line. Fortunately, it was much less expensive than the couture line, so younger women started to adopt the look.

The status of Le Smoking made it a cultural phenomenon. In 1971, Bianca Jagger wore a white version of the jacket at her wedding to Mick Jagger of the Rolling Stones, although she rocked it with a skirt instead of pants. Famed photographer Helmut Newton made the look even more iconic by doing a large layout for French Vogue in 1975. The images were powerful and daring, making the models who wore the look instant celebrities.

The Rive Gauche line was named after the location of the design shop, which was on the left bank of the River Seine. There, away from the places where he faced the pressures of creating high-end haute couture for the fashion house, Yves was free to be at his most creative, coming up with new looks and ideas for YSL.
The Le Smoking jacket is an important part of the history of YSL. It's always been a part of the line, even being included in Yves' final show that took place in 2002, and YSL still sells versions of it today. All the creative designers who came after Yves Saint Laurent himself designed updated variations that have rocked the YSL runways.

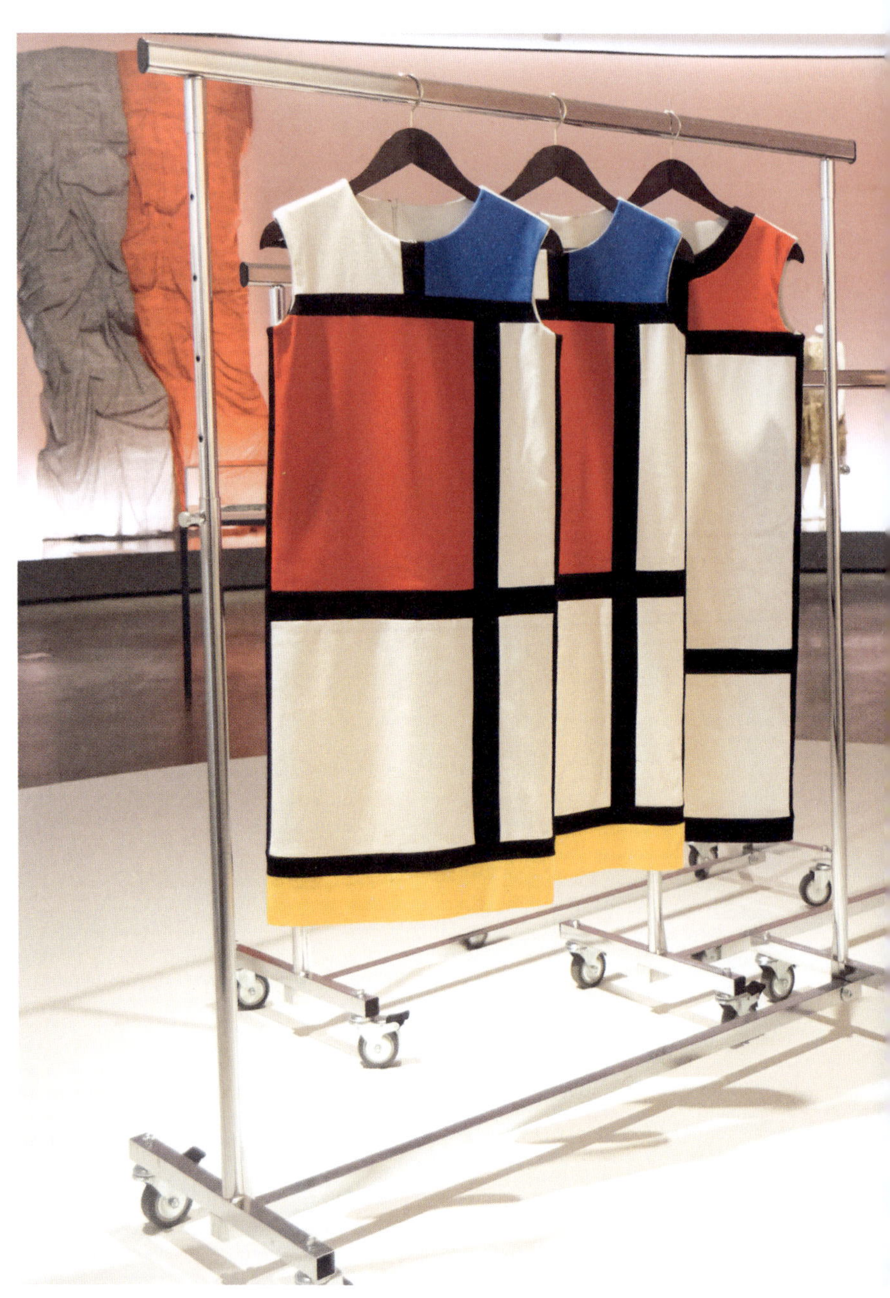

THE MONDRIAN DRESS

The Mondrian dress, created by Yves in 1965, was inspired by artist Piet Mondrian, whose work was characterized by giant blocks of color and geometrical shapes. Modern and grid-like, each of the six dresses in the collection featured this look. The Mondrian is considered a '60s-style shift dress without sleeves that is easy to wear and comfortable and has a gentle, comfortable shape. Once again, Yves produced an updated version of the Mondrian dress for his last show.

Mixing fashion with art was always on Yves' mind. In the Spring/Summer 1988 collection, he mixed certain pieces of art right into the clothing, using artists like Pablo Picasso, Henri Matisse, and Vincent Van Gogh.

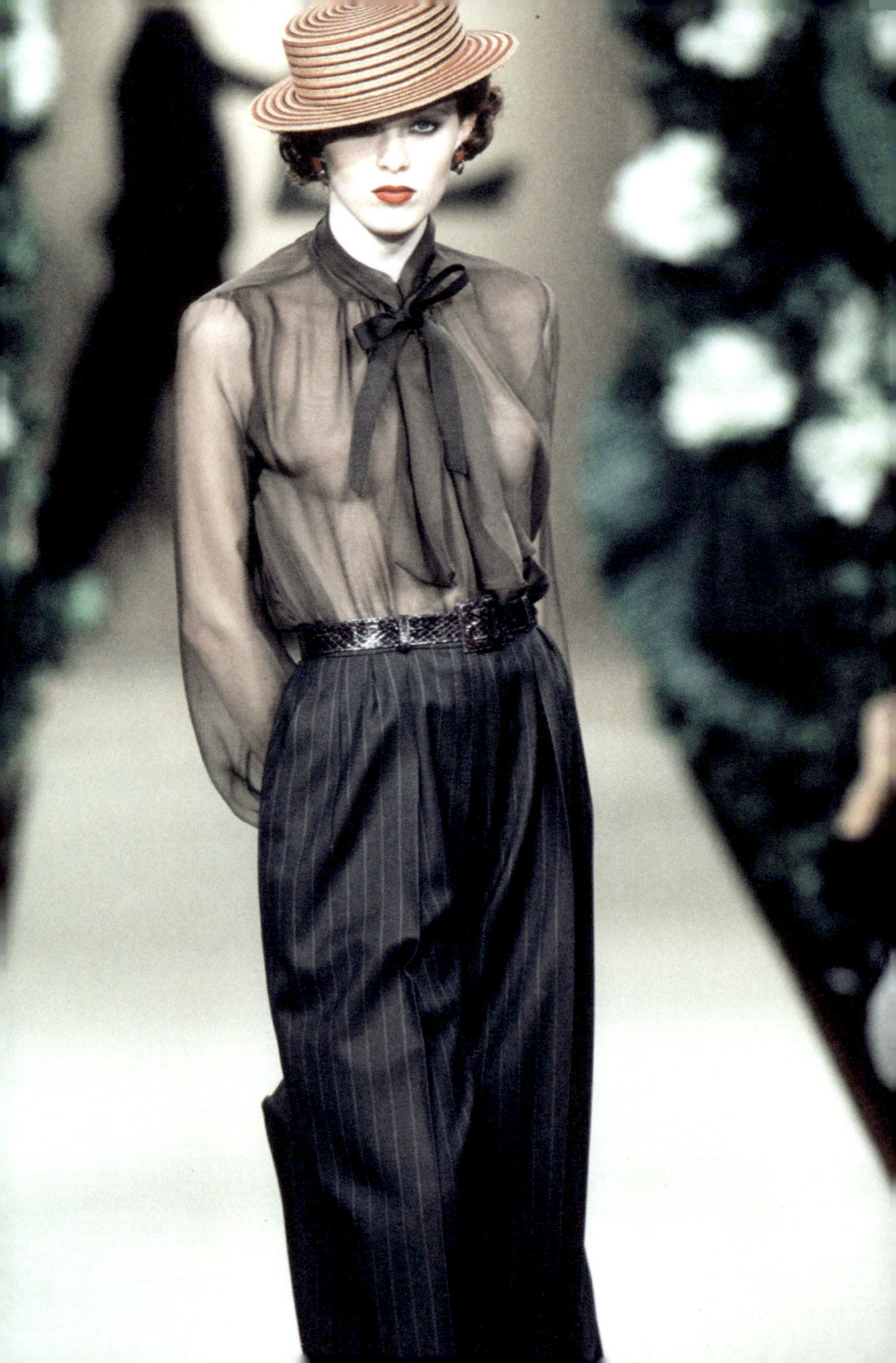

SHEER BLOUSES

Yves was always ahead of the time in everything he designed. Sheer blouses, which are sometimes referred to in popular culture as "freeing the nipple," are another look that he is well-known for creating. The sheer blouses and transparent chiffon dresses were classy and chic. These new looks were an ode to feminism in the 1960s, giving women the freedom to wear exactly what they wanted to wear. Yves once said, "Nothing is more beautiful than the naked body." Clearly, he was able to incorporate this idea into the elegant style of his clothing.

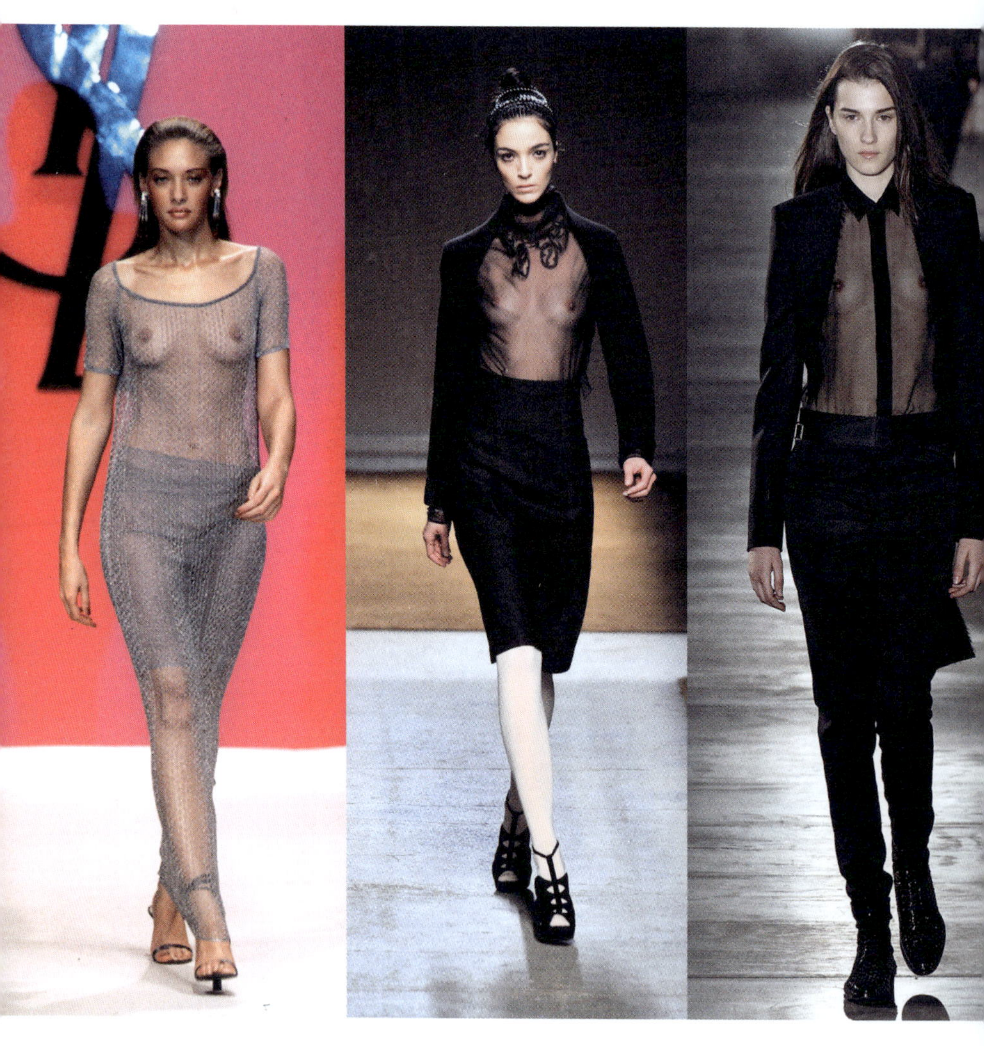

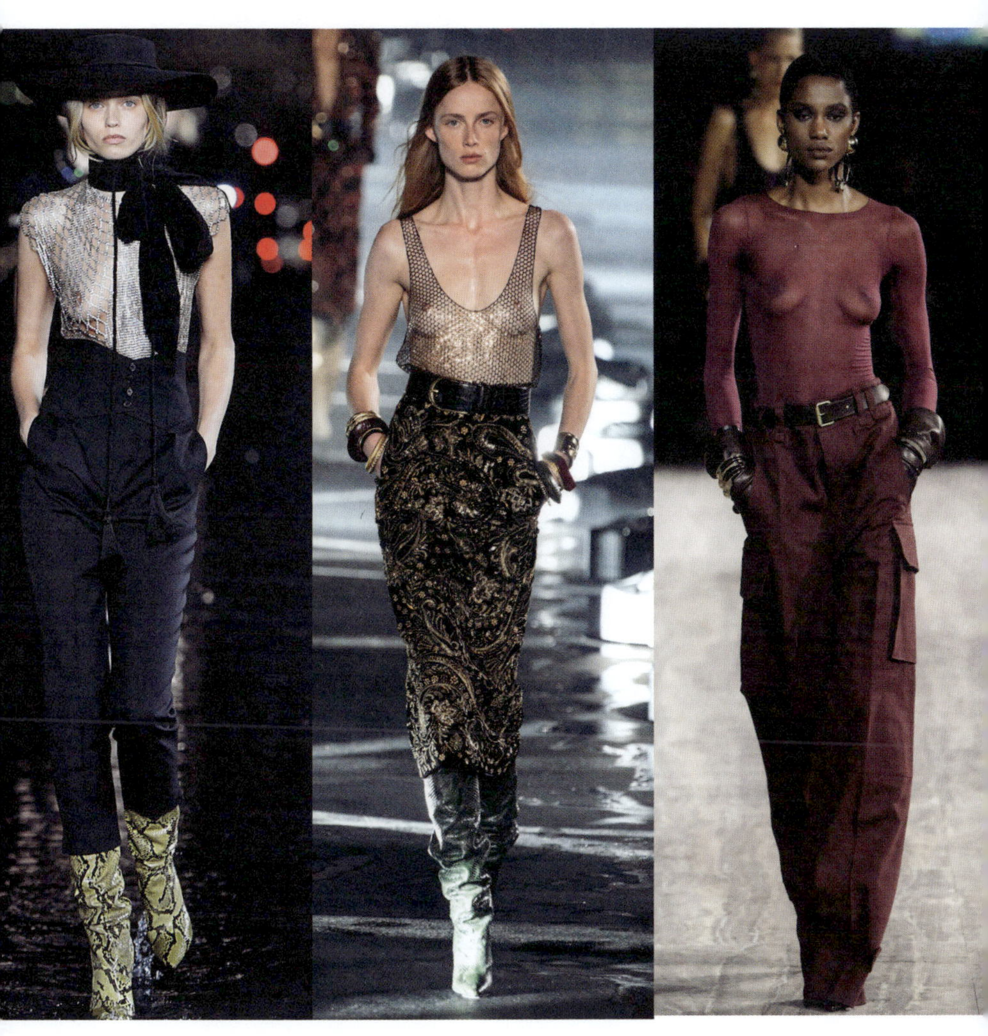

THE SAFARI JACKET

Finally, the Safari Jacket, designed in 1968, is another one of his most famous pieces. It's more a front-laced tunic than a jacket, and the design was a big hit for YSL. It became an instant sensation after it was photographed on model Veruschka von Lehndorff by famed photographer Franco Rubartelli for French Vogue. Decades later, the image was recreated in the 2009 issue of Harper's Bazaar, with supermodel Gisele Bunchon wearing a version of the jacket and striking the exact same pose as Veruschka.

So what is modern YSL clothing known for today? Under the direction of head designer Anthony Vaccarello, the designs have been sleek separates and updates of the classics that YSL is best known for. Here are some of the collections that have been a big hit in recent years.

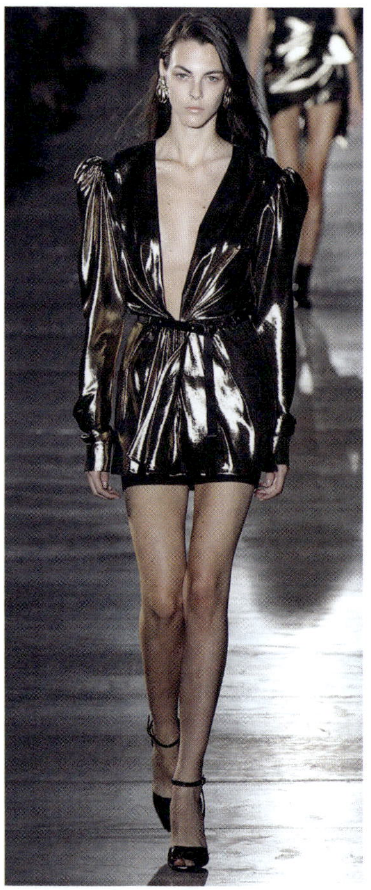

SPRING/ SUMMER *2017*

In almost all black, the edgy and modern look of the YSL dresses at this show was fantastic. Each dress was like a work of art, with interesting cut-outs, sheer lace fabrics, leather, and sequins. Beautiful and elegant.

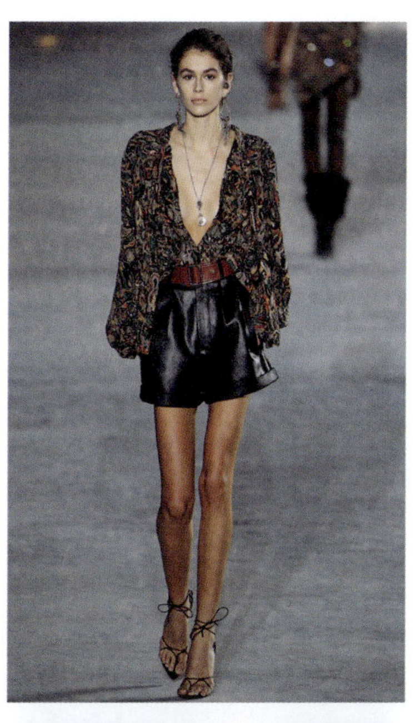

SPRING/ SUMMER *2018*

The following year, in Spring/Summer 2018, Anthony veered toward even more edgy designs. Dark fabrics and eye-catching accessories were easily worn by the models in looks that could only be described as outrageously elegant.

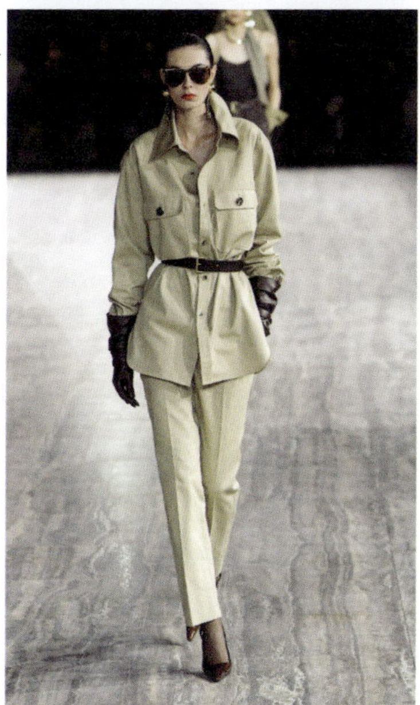

SPRING/ SUMMER *2024*

Most of Anthony's collections for YSL have had a lot of interesting details and embroidery, but for the Spring/Summer 2024 collection, he went in the opposite direction, stripping everything back to basics. He wanted a clean canvas and a fresh start for YSL. Basing most of the line on the famous Safari Jacket, he reworked the jacket to take away the lace-up closure and give it a simpler look. There were jumpsuits, pencil skirts, and shirtdresses with few embellishments. It was his version of the trend that is "quiet luxury." The collection was pretty and basic but actually a tad boring, according to fashion editors that season.

“YVES SAINT LAURENT’S IMPACT ON FASHION IS *IMMEASURABLE*. HE WAS A TRUE ARTIST AND INNOVATOR.”

Claudia Schiffer

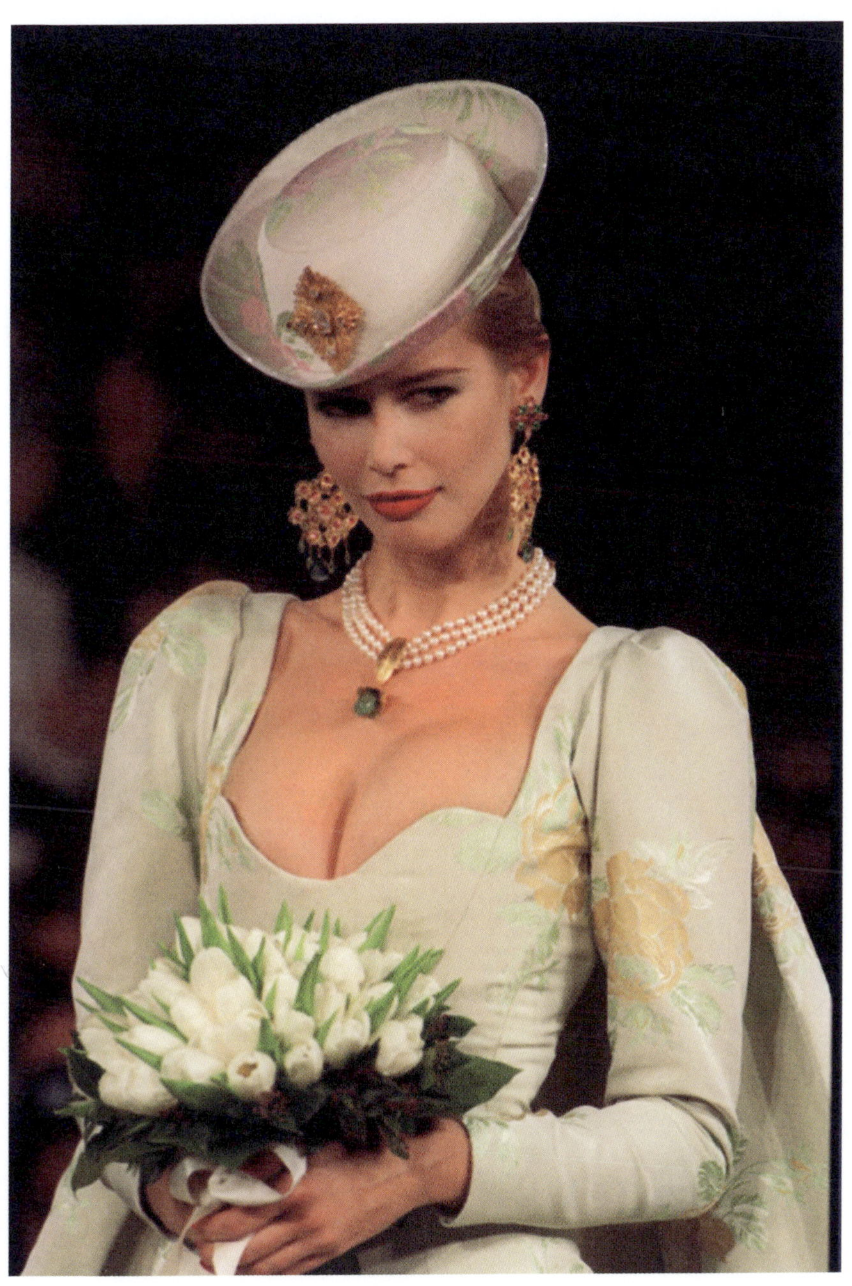

5

SAC DU JOUR, LOULOU, *and* MORE

Handbags

THE GOLD-TONED HARDWARE OF THE YSL LETTERING across a luxury handbag is unmistakable. Yet, it's funny that during the '60s and '70s, when Yves Saint Laurent started releasing handbags, they were produced without a lot of thought. Yves didn't really care much about the handbag line, unlike many other fashion houses, especially Gucci, Hermes, and Louis Vuitton. For Yves, YSL's handbags were an afterthought.

The early handbags were made from materials like snakeskin, Moroccan leather, and even tortoise skin. Madame Perrin and Madame Leroux were the two ladies responsible for designing the handbags. Most of the original bags were pretty boring and boxy looking, with gold chains that came from jewelry lines the company no longer sold. Still, several of the bags were released with some success, like the Sac du Jour, the LouLou, and the Kaia bag. Today, handbags are a huge part of YSL's overall business, and the company releases many special editions and reboots in a variety of colors and materials. Here are some of the most popular YSL handbags over time.

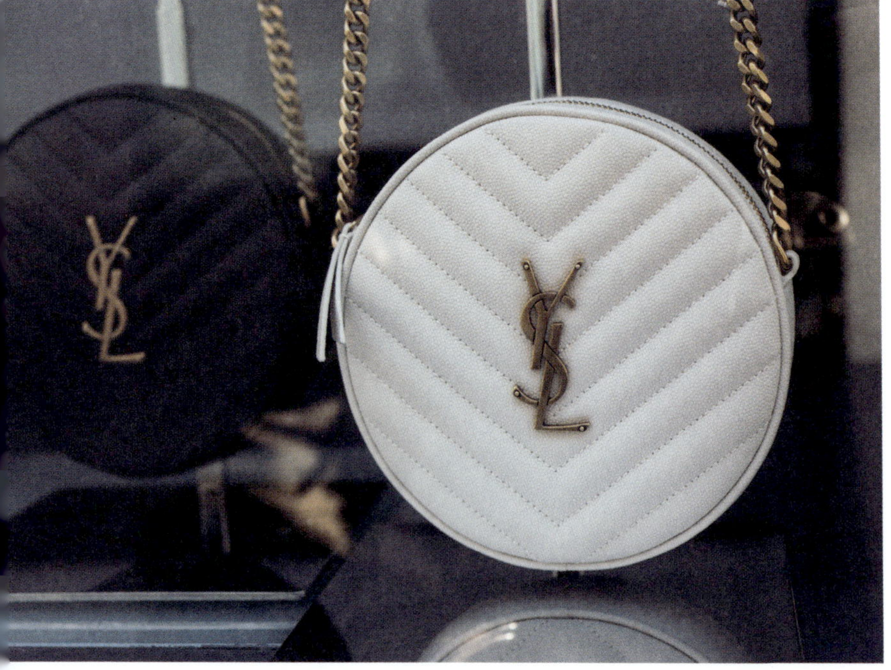

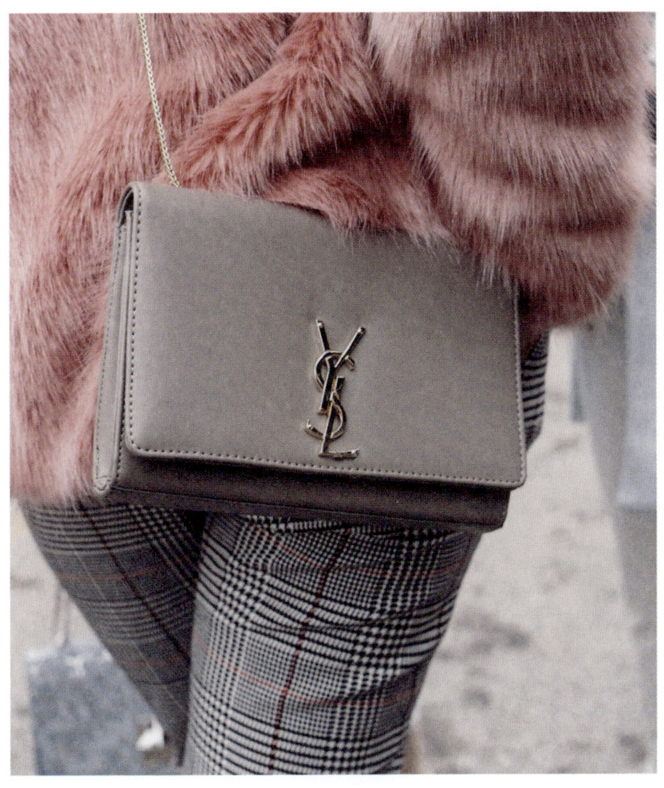

KATE

The Kate, introduced in 2010 and named after supermodel Kate Moss, is one of the most iconic handbags ever introduced by YSL. It's still a popular bag sold today, with its flap style, gold chain hardware, and large YSL initial logo on the front. Some of the bags even have a snazzy tassel that hangs down from the logo. Even though its style is basic, it is produced in a ton of different colors and fabric variations, so if you get bored with one of yours but still love the shape, you can always go for a completely different version. Many people do.

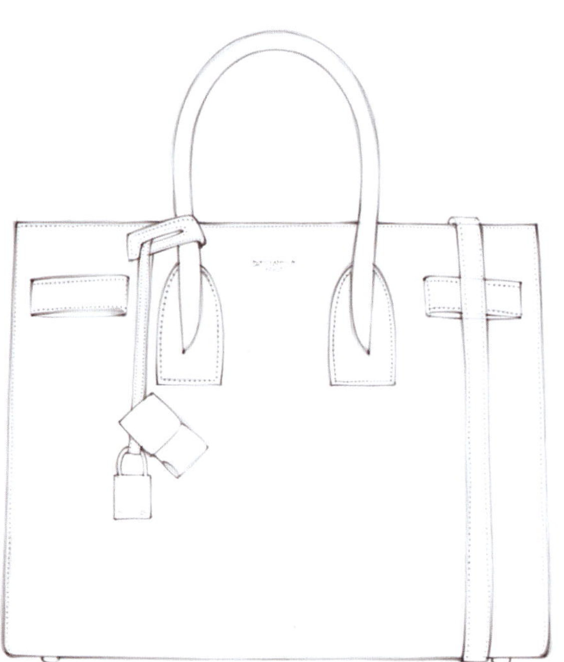

SAC DU JOUR

The YSL Sac du Jour came out in 2013, when Hedi Slimane was creative director. The name means "bag of the day." It's meant to be the bag you carry all your essentials in every day. It has a simple top handle and a square design, and it comes in a variety of sizes—nano, baby, small, and large. This bag looks very similar to another famous handbag, the Hermes Birkin bag. Maybe that's why it's so popular. Or it could be the fact that it's a very versatile and functional bag for daily use.

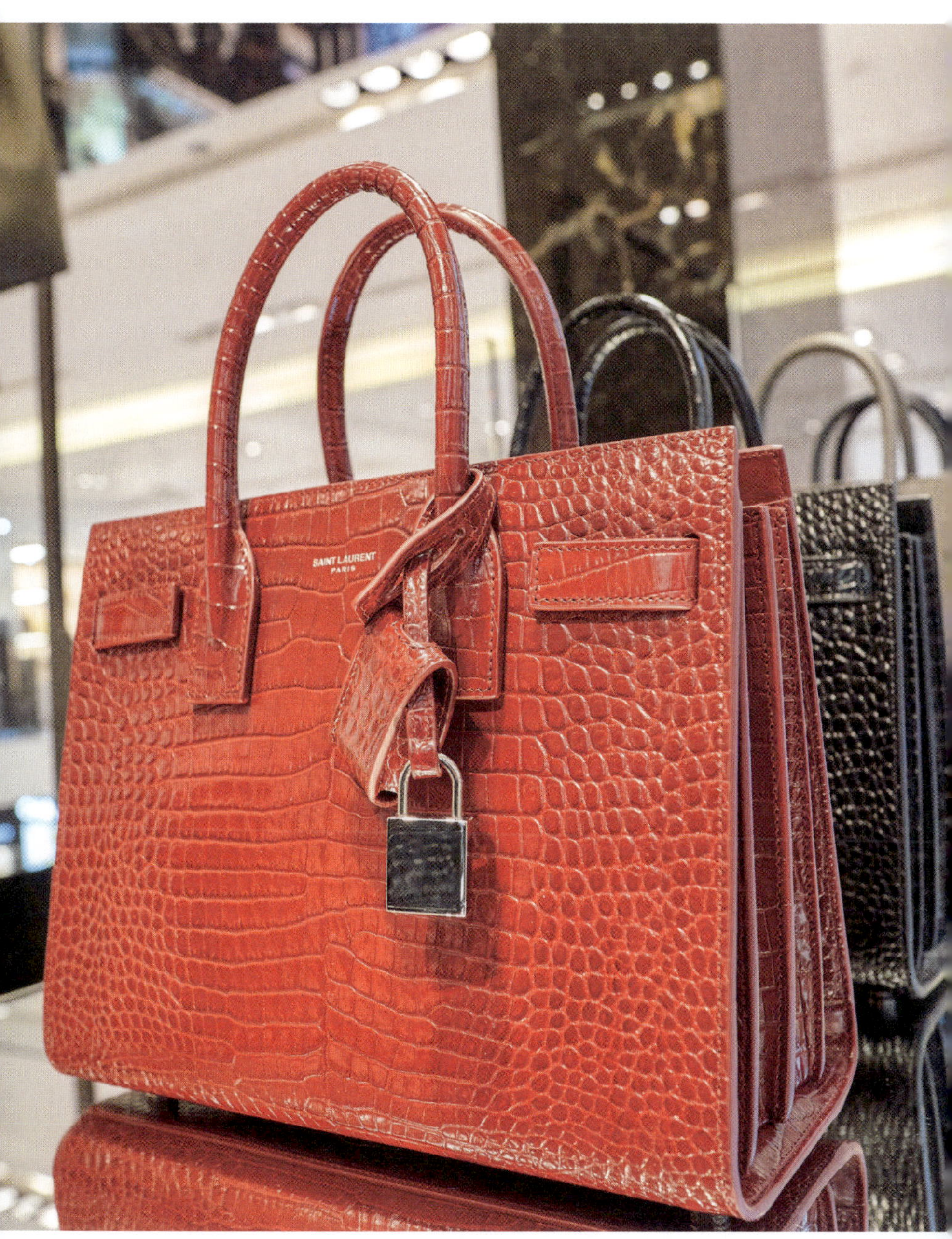
SAINT LAURENT
PARIS

CALYPSO

The Calypso is another bag that came out in 2013. A shoulder bag with gold chain hardware, it has the overall aesthetic that most of the YSL bags tend to have, but that doesn't make it any less luxe and exciting. The Calypso has a slightly elongated shape with the YSL logo prominently featured on the front. Right now, it's only sold in two different sizes, small and large, but watch out for new revamps of it because it seems to be popular for the line that's featured by name alongside the Jamie and the Le 5 à 7 in the handbag section on the YSL website. All the other bags can be found under "other lines."

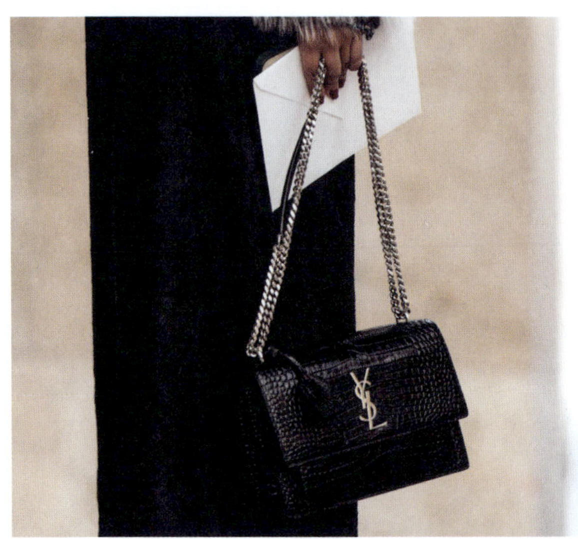

SUNSET

The Sunset came out in 2016 in small, medium, and large. It comes with a double chain with leather at the top of the strap and is either a crossbody or shoulder bag, depending on the length of the adjustable chain. The rectangular flap bag, like most of YSL's offerings, has the YSL logo right on the front. The medium style is the most popular, and it comes in 14 different variations of fabrics and colors. You're bound to find one that will become your absolute favorite.

LOULOU

If you want a bag that looks as soft as a pillow, Loulou is the one for you. It's made of a quilted, almost puffy-looking leather (chevron quilted), with a gold chain and leather strap that allows it to be worn as a shoulder or crossbody bag. The Loulou came out in 2017, and it currently comes in four different sizes: toy crossbody, small, medium, and large crossbody. Anthony Vaccarello was the creative director who released this bag, and he named it after a long-time muse of Yves Saint Laurent, Loulou de la Falaise. It's been one of YSL's best-selling handbags since it was released.

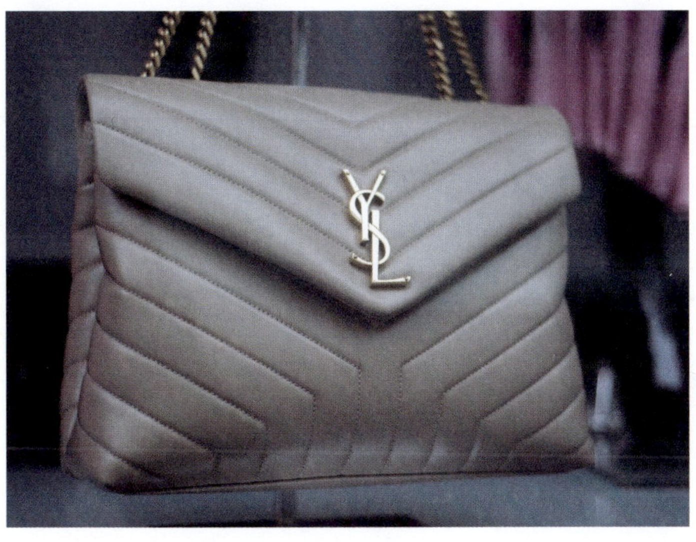

JAMIE

Another new arrival is the Jamie bag, which came out in Spring 2018. Its style is similar to that of many of the YSL bags, with gold chain hardware, a large YSL logo, and a flap-style closure. It's sold in a number of different sizes, including mini, small, medium, and even a Jamie 4.3 in lambskin that comes in a larger size. With classic or patent leather, the different colors are nice over basic black, cream, or brown. The "Rouge Merlot" is a particularly striking color for fall and would stand out over some of your other basic bags.

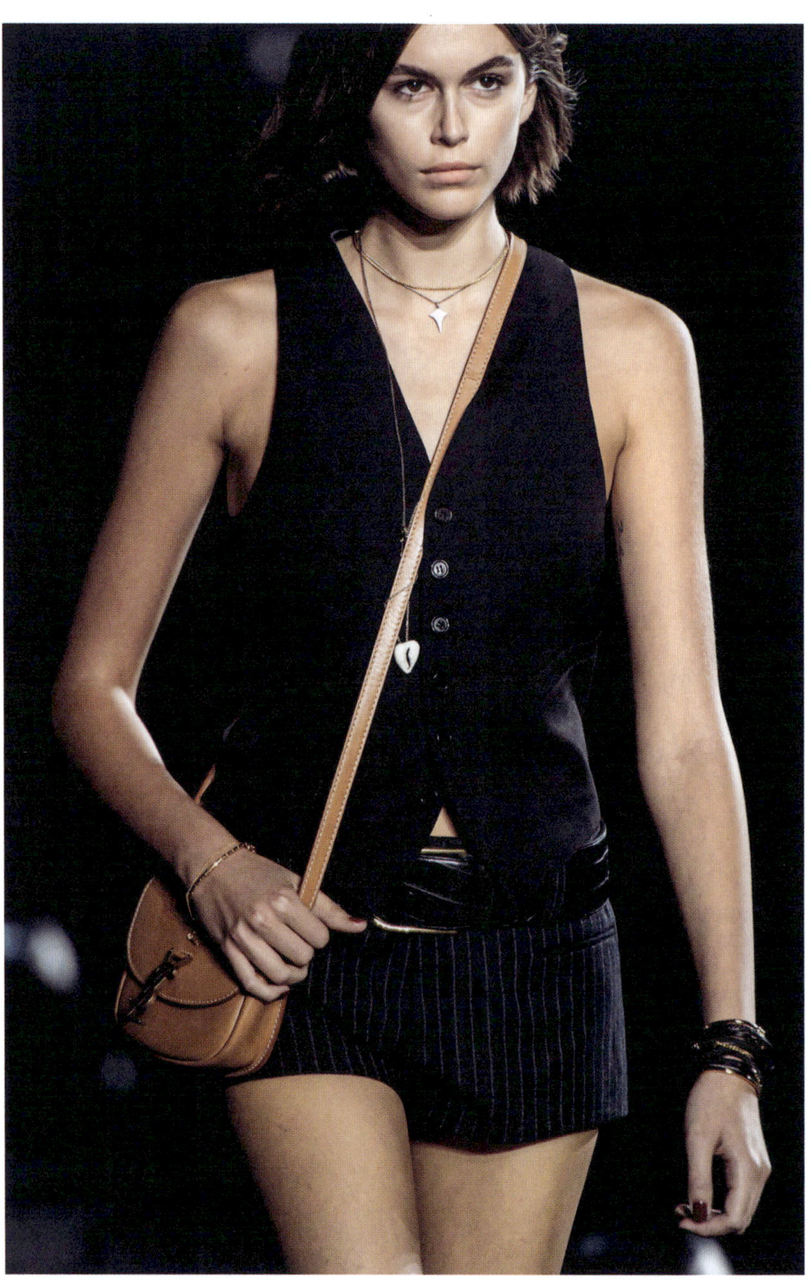

KAIA

Spring/Summer 2020 brought a modern and new handbag from YSL called the Kaia. It was named after model Kaia Gerber, the daughter of famed supermodel Cindy Crawford. It immediately earned cult status, simply because so many "It Girl" celebrities, like Hailey Bieber, Lucy Boynton, and Blackpink's Rosé, carry it around daily. It is a small satchel-style bag with a large YSL logo in gold hardware on the front, easy to carry around crossbody. For extra luxury, buy it in the shiny crocodile-embossed leather.

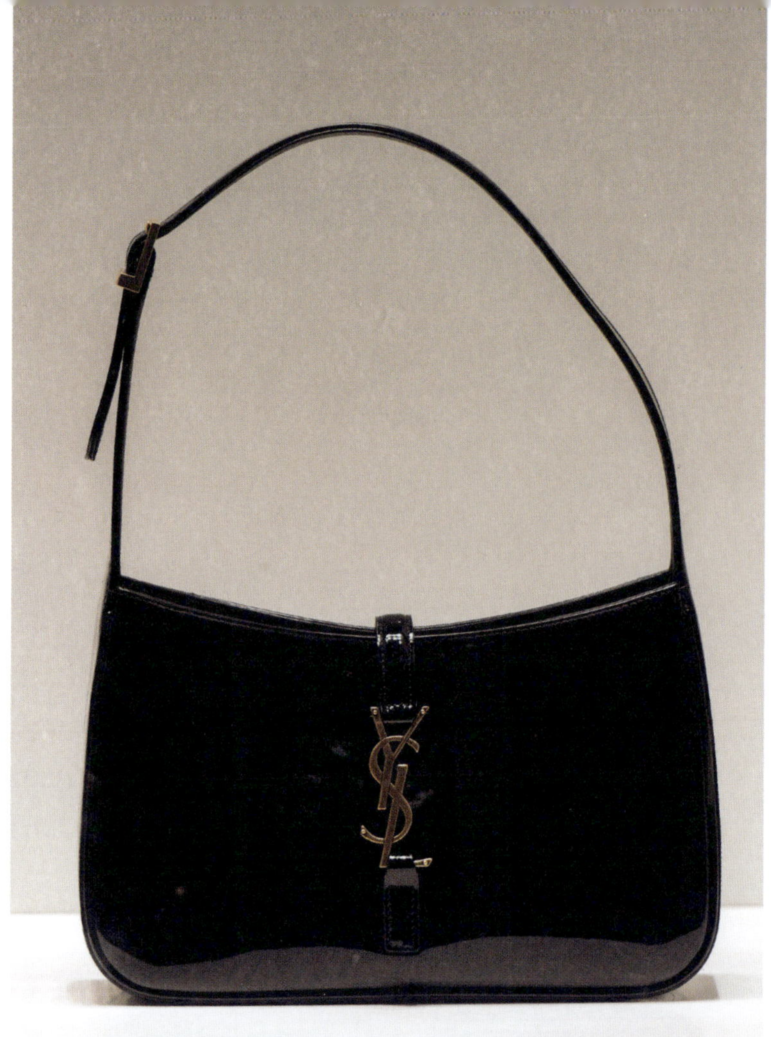

LE 5 À 7

Spring 2021 brought along the Le 5 à 7 handbag. As a hobo-style shoulder bag, it was a fun style with the YSL logo initials in a smaller font near the closure on the front. It is still sold today in different sizes and in smooth, grained leather, canvas, raffia, and even suede. Why do they call it the Le 5 à 7? The current creative director, Anthony Vaccarello, named it after his favorite French cult-classic movie, Cleo from 5 to 7, which came out in 1962 and is about a young female singer on a quest to find herself.

ICARE

The Icare maxi shopping bag has an interesting shape. It is the perfect quilted handbag that looks like a large triangle with a small handle and a very large gold-tone YSL logo on the front. It comes in quilted suede, quilted nubuck leather, or raffia for a more casual look. It came out in 2002, and celebrities such as Sydney Sweeney, Zoe Kravitz, and Miley Cyrus have been seen with it. The name has a funny story to it. Anthony Vaccarello said the name came from the large gold logo letters that are so bright in the center of the bag that they "shine like the sun that burnt the wings of Icarus." So, "Icare" was born.

LE 37

The Le 37 is a classic bucket bag that comes in a mini, small, and regular size. It's named after the Paris address, 37 Rue de Bellechasse. The logo is small, and at the top of the bag is a metal Cassandre hook closure. There is a top handle and a longer strap to carry the bag crossbody. There is plenty of room in every size of this bag—you could even throw a water bottle in there while traveling. The bag was reissued in 2023, with K-Pop idol Rosé, from the group Blackpink, being pictured with this signature bucket bag as part of the advertising campaign.

RIVE GAUCHE TOTE

Rive Gauche is YSL's ready-to-wear line, so it makes sense that some handbags are part of this line. This is a basic shopping tote with the words "Rive Gauche Saint Laurent" emblazoned on it—a cult status item if there ever was one. Currently, it comes in many different sizes and colors, but the must-have vacation bag is made of wicker-like raffia that comes in a light tan. It's the ideal bag for holding your book, sunscreen, water bottle, and towel to take to the beach.

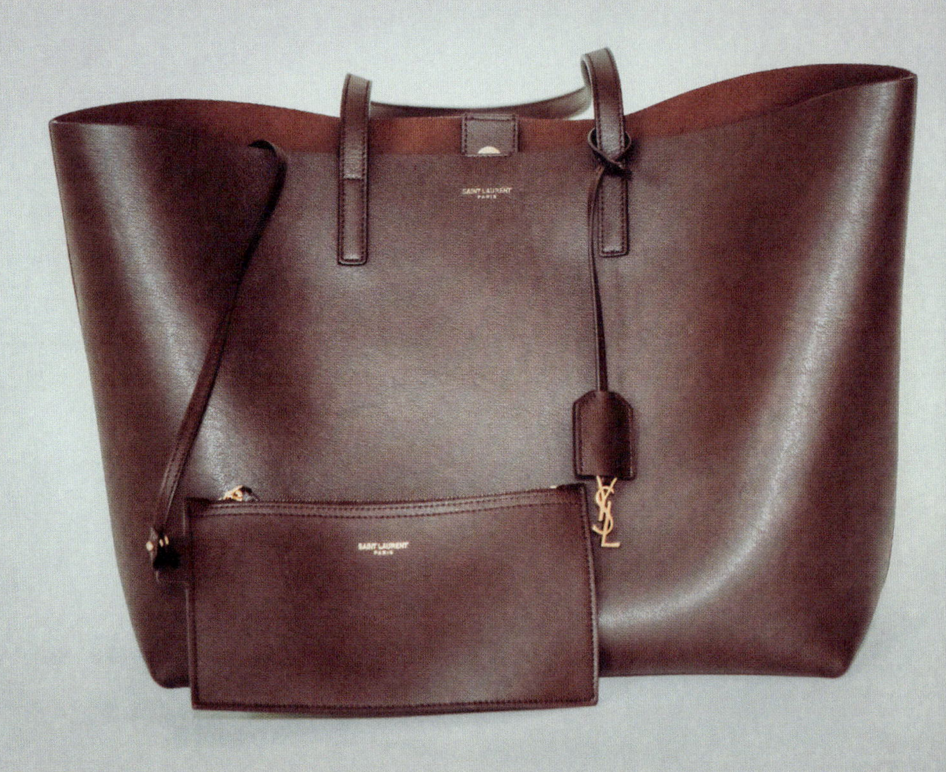

SHOPPING TOTE

For a less casual shopping bag, there is the YSL Shopping Tote. It has the logo, "Saint Laurent" in very tiny letters at the top. This is a quiet luxury handbag and a tote that is great to take to work. It will easily hold a laptop, tablet, and anything else you may need for the day. You can get it in practically any color of leather you would like, but "Navy" and "Dark Green" are very chic and are a nice change from basic black or brown.

"I LOVE YSL BECAUSE THEIR DESIGNS ARE BOTH EDGY AND TIMELESS. THEY'RE THE PERFECT BLEND OF MODERN AND CLASSIC."

Hailey Bieber

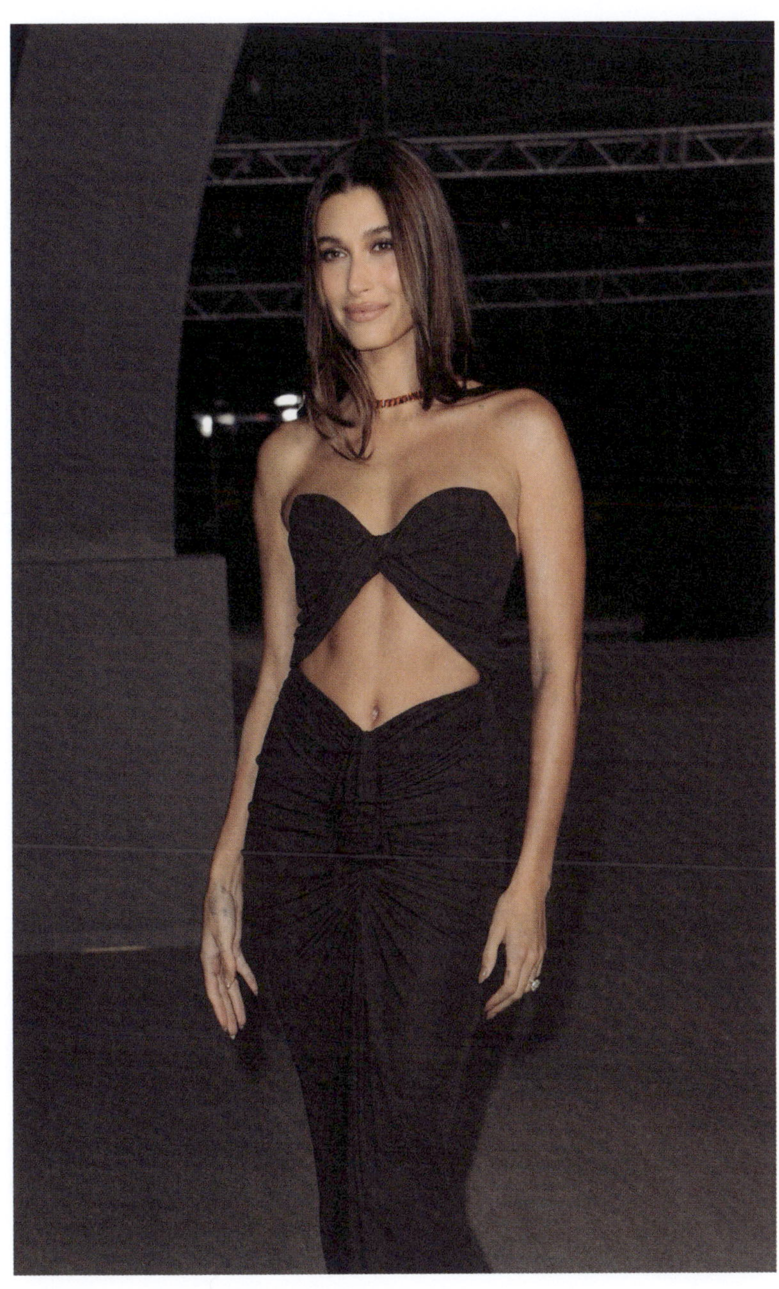

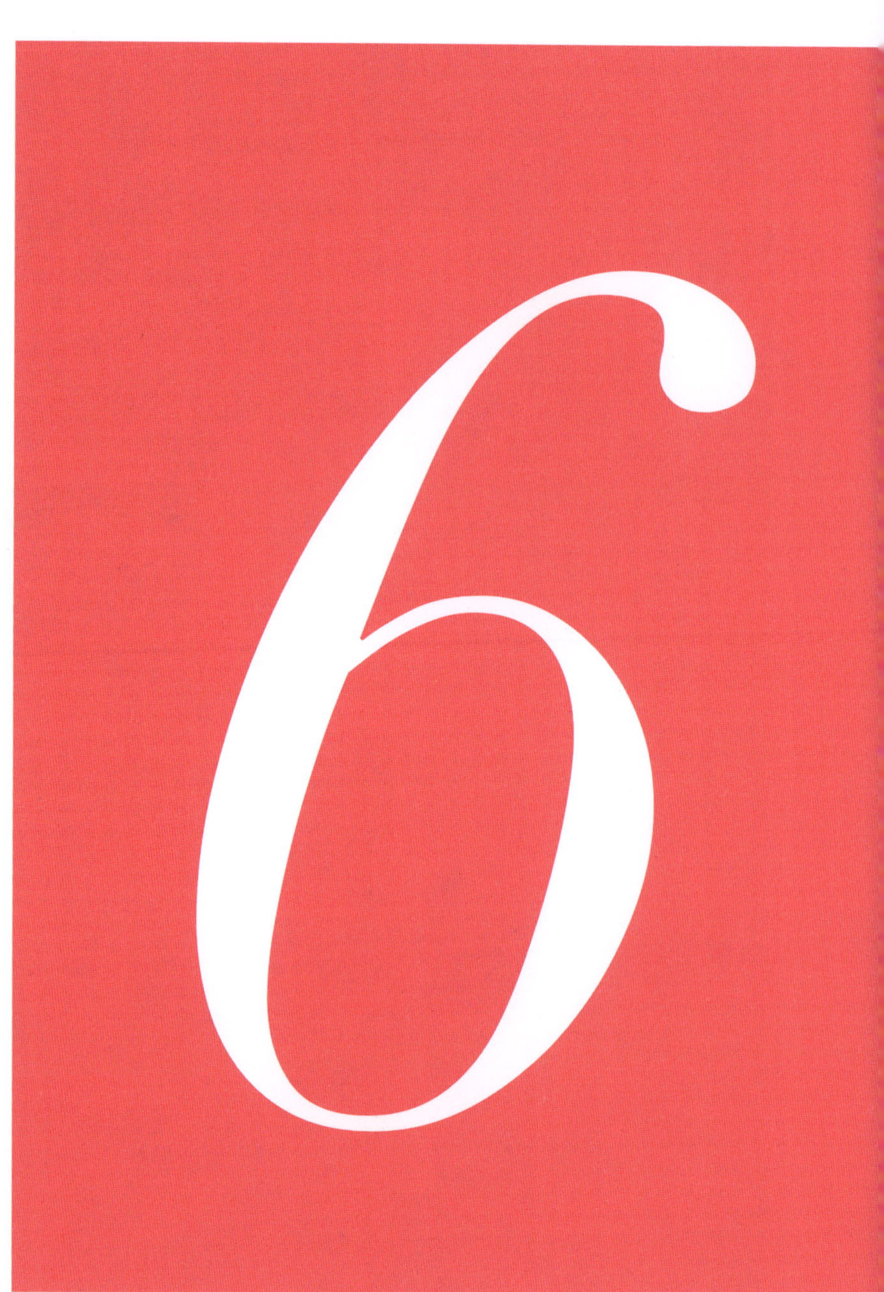
6

JEWELRY, SHOES, and COSMETICS

Accessories

YSL HAS GORGEOUS HAUTE COUTURE, beautiful ready-to-wear, iconic handbags, and many other luxury items. Three of the top sellers in these other categories are jewelry, shoes, and cosmetics. Let's consider the history of how these items came to be part of the House of Saint Laurent and look at some of the best-sellers today.

JEWELRY
in the 1960s and 1970s

The first YSL jewelry collection was launched in 1965, with Yves Saint Laurent creating it to go with the ready-to-wear line available at that time. His designs were inspired by his travels to different places, including China, Africa, and India. Many of the patterns and symbols used were cultural references to these places, and bright colors and interesting shapes were used to create a bold effect. The items were made of enamel, glass, and different types of leather, which was quite revolutionary and a unique departure from what was popular at the time. The mixing of natural materials with man-made materials made this African 67 collection incredibly diverse.

The 1975 Coral collection was another popular jewelry collection in the early days of the fashion house. Gold, silver, and precious stones were used in designs that featured things from nature, such as flowers and leaves. The large, chunky pieces were creative and colorful, which made the jewelry the focal point of any look. Bohemian chic is a great way to describe how this jewelry looks when worn.

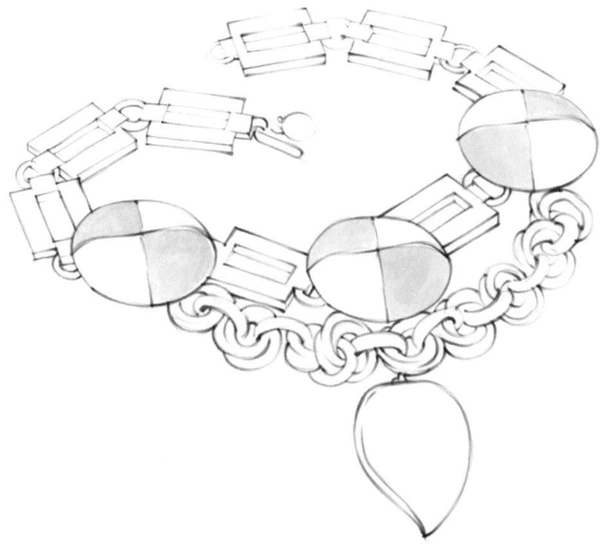

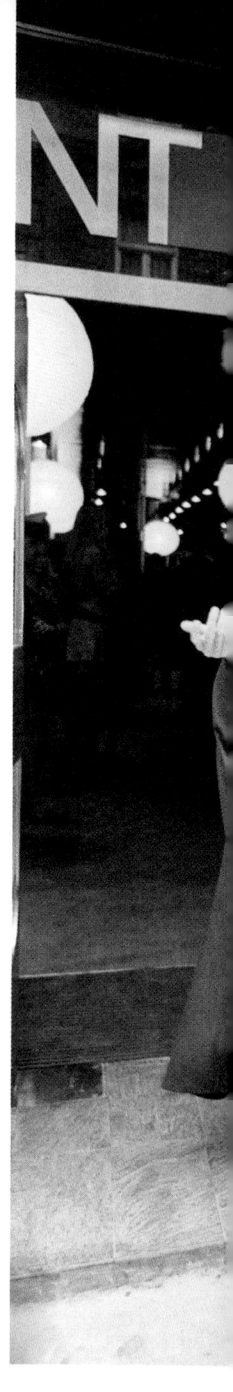

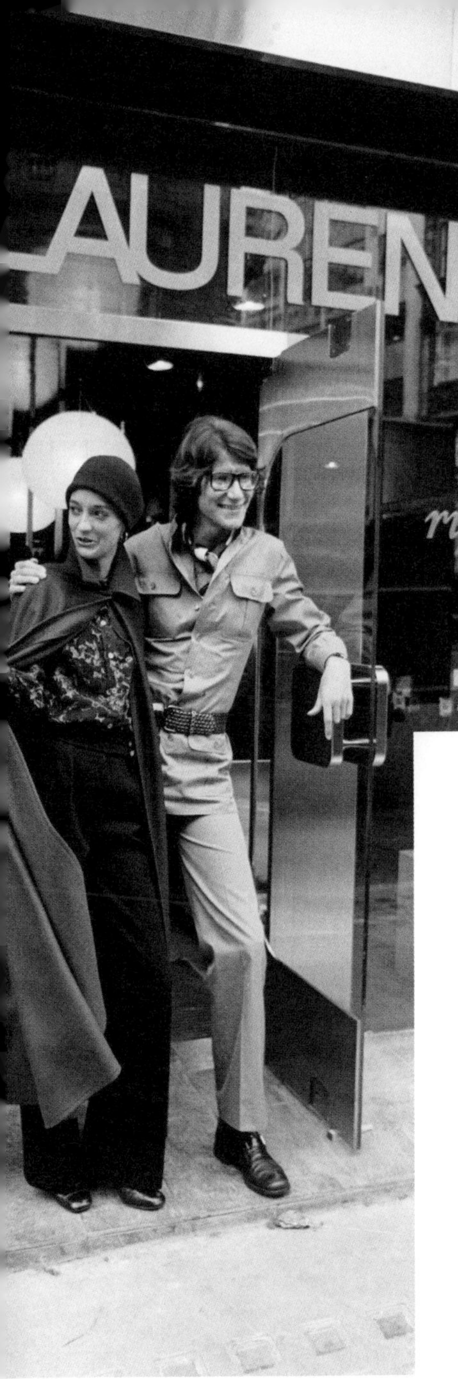

LOULOU
The LouLou bracelet is named after Yves Saint Laurent's muse, Louise de La Falaise, who was known as LouLou.

The Loulou necklace, one of the most iconic pieces, was inspired by his model friend Loulou de la Falaise. It consisted of an oversized gold chain with a pendant-style tassel on the front and smaller, delicate gold chains hanging down. She was rarely seen without this gorgeous necklace.

The Opium necklace was another cool '70s piece of jewelry that became very popular. It had a similar tassel to the Loulou necklace but with more beads, crystals, and pearls attached to it. Yves' very good movie star friend, Catherine Deneuve, wore it in an ad for the Opium fragrance.

Other fun pieces from the 1970s include the Cage necklace and the Muse bracelet. The Muse wrapped around the wrist like a piece of armor, and the Cage had a large geometric pendant made from gold wire. All these pieces were oversized, thoughtful, and memorable.

JEWELRY
in the 1980s and 1990s

The '80s were all about glamour and decadence, and the jewelry that YSL produced during this decade continued to be bold and adventurous. All the styles reflected the over-the-top trends at the time. One of the best pieces that YSL produced in the '80s was the Belle de Jour bracelet, which was inspired by the 1967 film of the same name. This was probably the most minimalist piece that had been produced up to that point. The Belle de Jour was a simple gold bangle that had a clasp adorned with the YSL logo.

The YSL Tassel necklace also came out at this time. It had the same style that is used on the closure of a lot of different handbags made by the fashion house. The Tassel necklace featured a large pendant, with smaller gold chains that ended with crystals and pearls on the tassel. It was more delicate and prettier than previous designs had been.

Yves continued to explore the different ways in which interesting materials—including resin, wood, and cloth —could be used as part of his jewelry collections. The Cubist collection used a lot of plastic resin, lacquered wood, and different metals in big bold shapes, and the Matisse collection was just as colorful and abstract.

The 1990s saw the production of YSL jewelry collections that featured the logo more prominently. In the '90s, logos were very big, so lots of necklaces, bracelets, and rings just featured the YSL logo in simple designs. Statement cuffs were big, chunky chains, and the Maison collection, launched in 1992, was created to pay tribute to the design of the house's logo. Overall, YSL jewelry was always ahead of its time when Yves was behind its creation.

GOLD
American actress Zaria Simone arrives at the Red Carpet adorned in YSL jewelry.

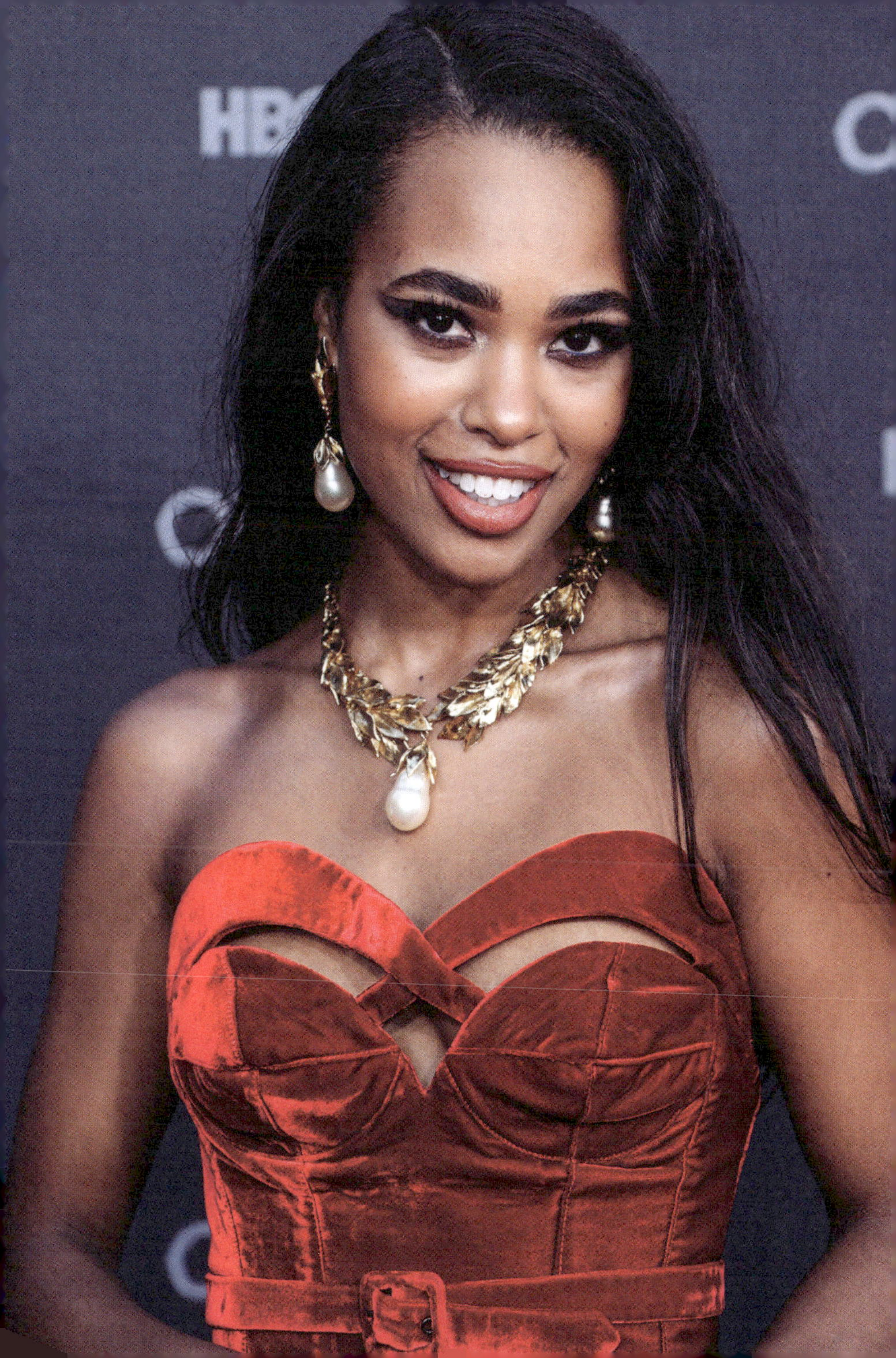

SHOES

Yves Saint Laurent's accessories have always been legendary, including the shoes that he came out with to complement the line. One of the first pairs he designed was for the Fall/Winter collection of 1965. Catherine Deneuve wore a pair in the movie Belle du Jour. This shoe was a low-heeled, patent-leather shoe with a large silver buckle, and it quickly became a YSL classic. Roger Vivier, a famous shoemaker at the time, helped Yves make his shoe designs come to life.

Today, YSL makes all types of shoes, including flats, boots, loafers, pumps, slingbacks, and even sneakers. No matter what kind of shoe you need for an outfit, you'll find a gorgeous pair to wear. Some of the current most popular and best-selling styles are the Nour slippers, Monceau pumps, Dune slingback pumps, and Babylone sandals, which are strappy, lace-up high heels. Very sexy.

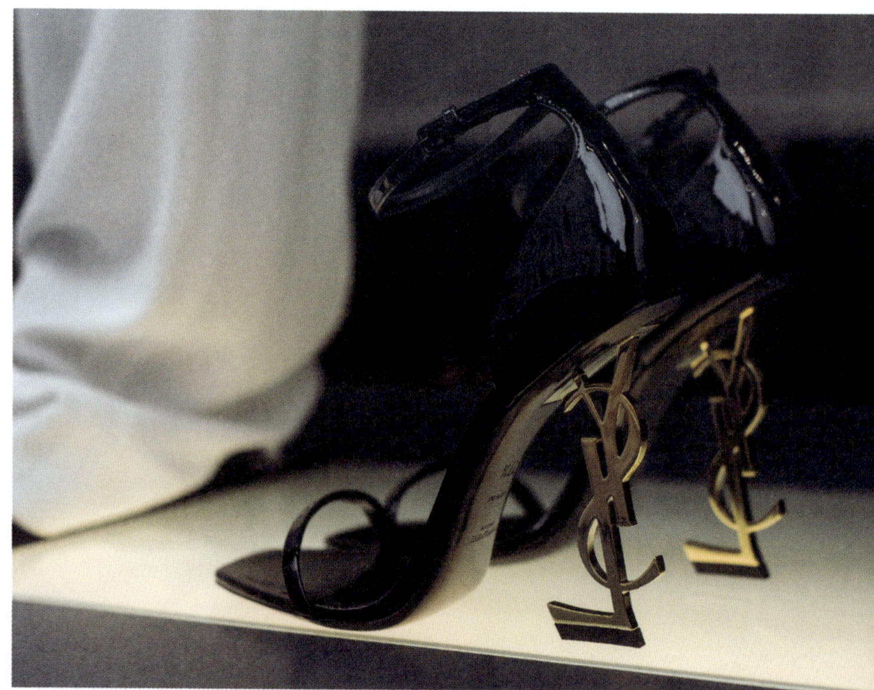

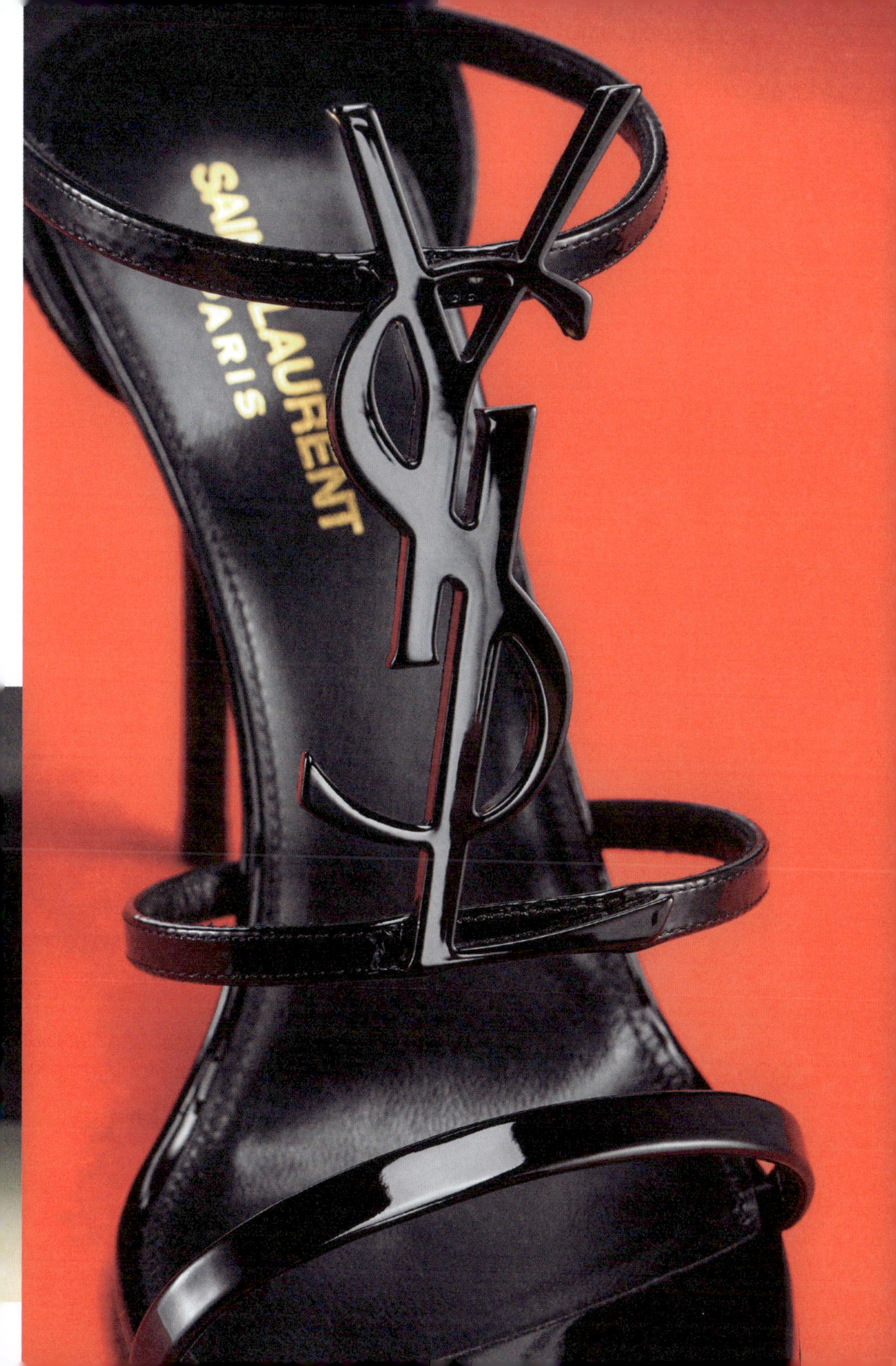
LAURENT

COSMETICS

YSL Beauty kicked off with a fragrance in 1964, eventually leading to the creation of a beauty line in 1978. The first beauty item introduced was a line of lipstick in predominantly red and fuchsia. The Rouge Pur No. 19 was one of the first lipsticks and is still made to this day, having become one of the company's most popular shades, a blue–red fuchsia. Yves thought that every great outfit needed the perfect lipstick to go with it. Bold. Unique. Statement-making.

Today, YSL Beauty makes a full line of makeup and skincare products in addition to its popular fragrance offerings. The company is now owned by cosmetics mega-giant L'Oréal, and its global president is Stephen Bezy. Here are some of the best-selling YSL Beauty products.

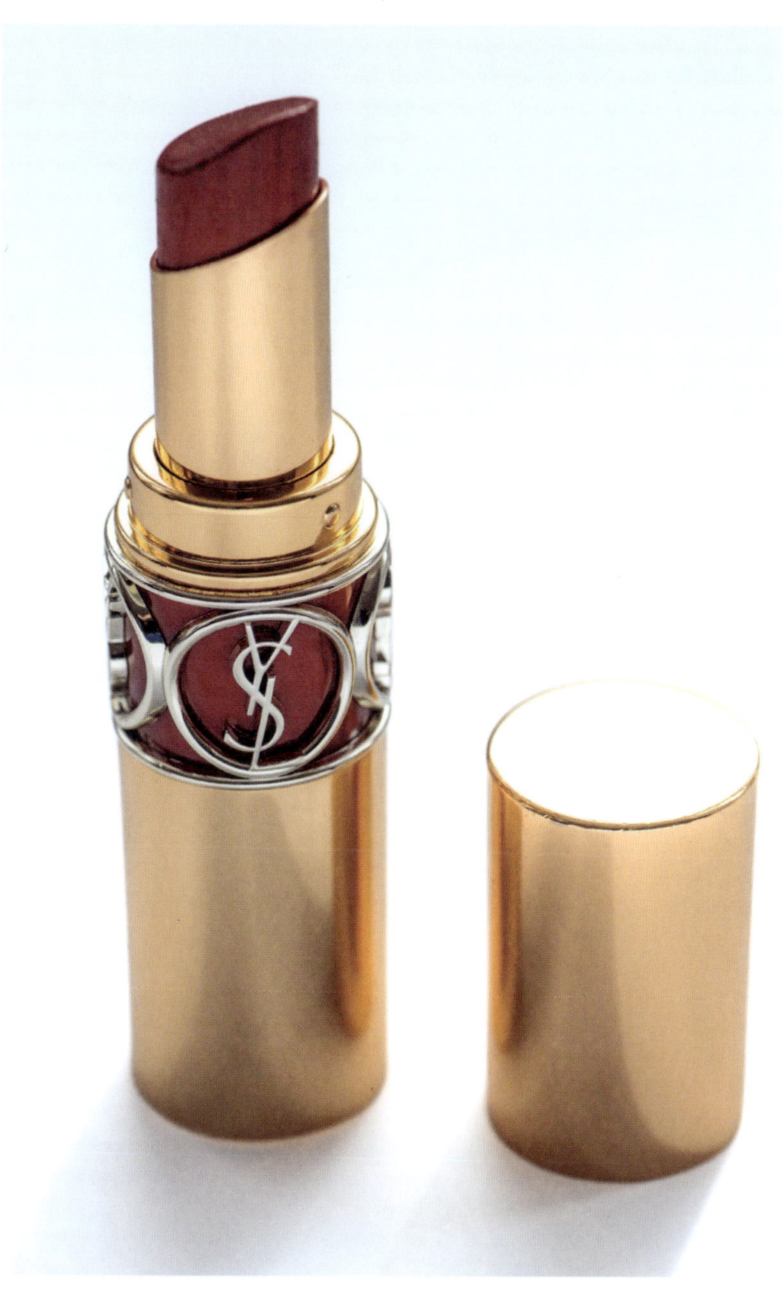

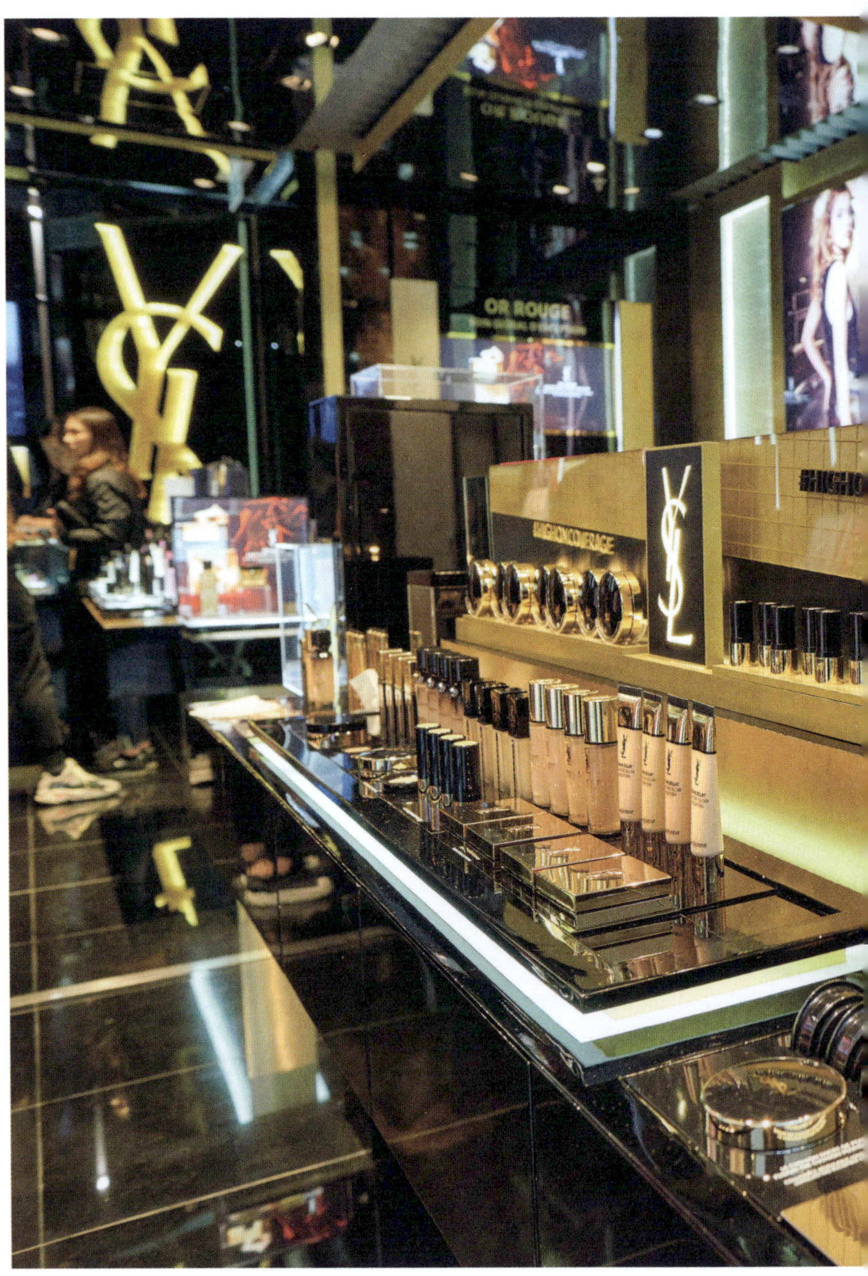
OR ROUGE
#HIGHONCOVERAGE

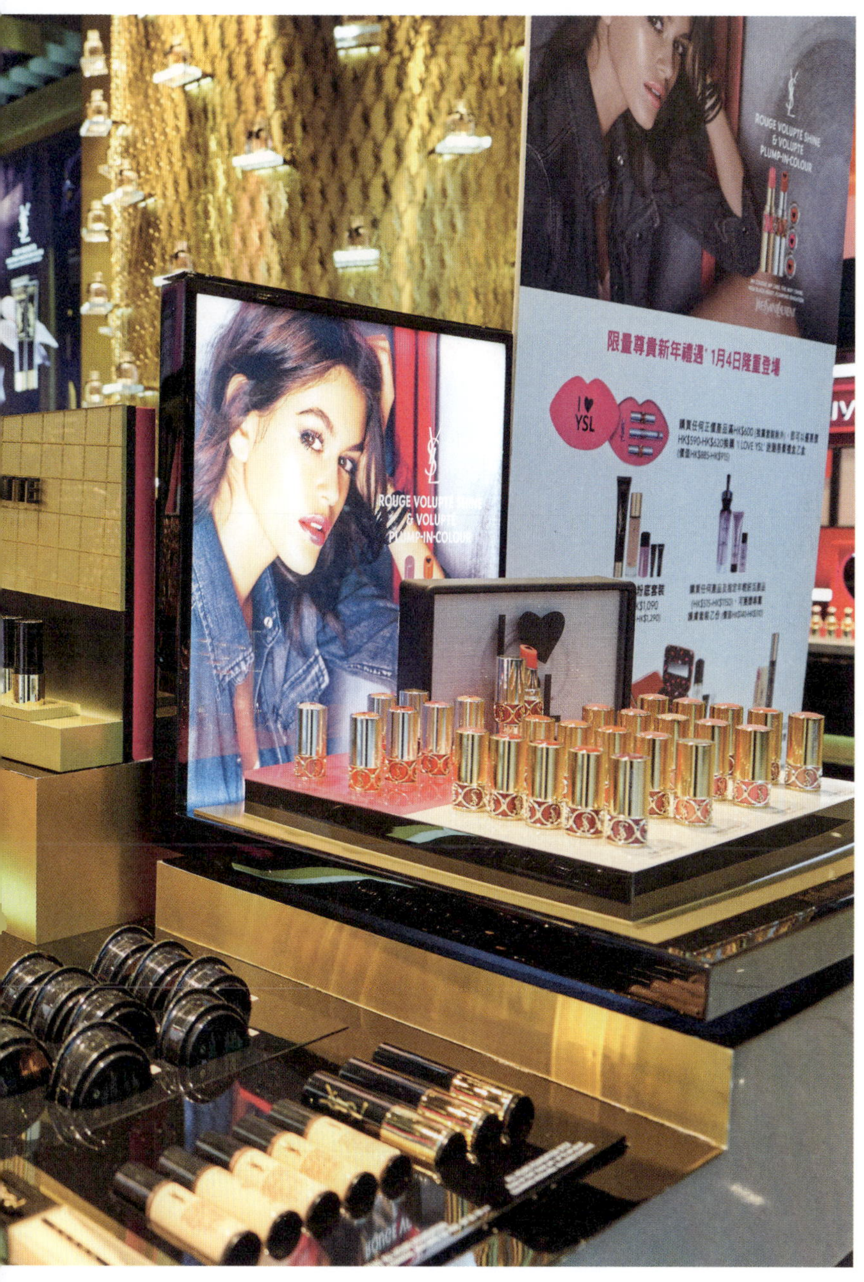
ROUGE VOLUPTE SHINE
& VOLUPTE
PLUMP-IN-COLOUR
ROUGE VOLUPTE
& VOLUPTE
PLUMP-IN-COLOUR
限量尊貴新年禮遇* 1月4日隆重登場
I ♥ YSL

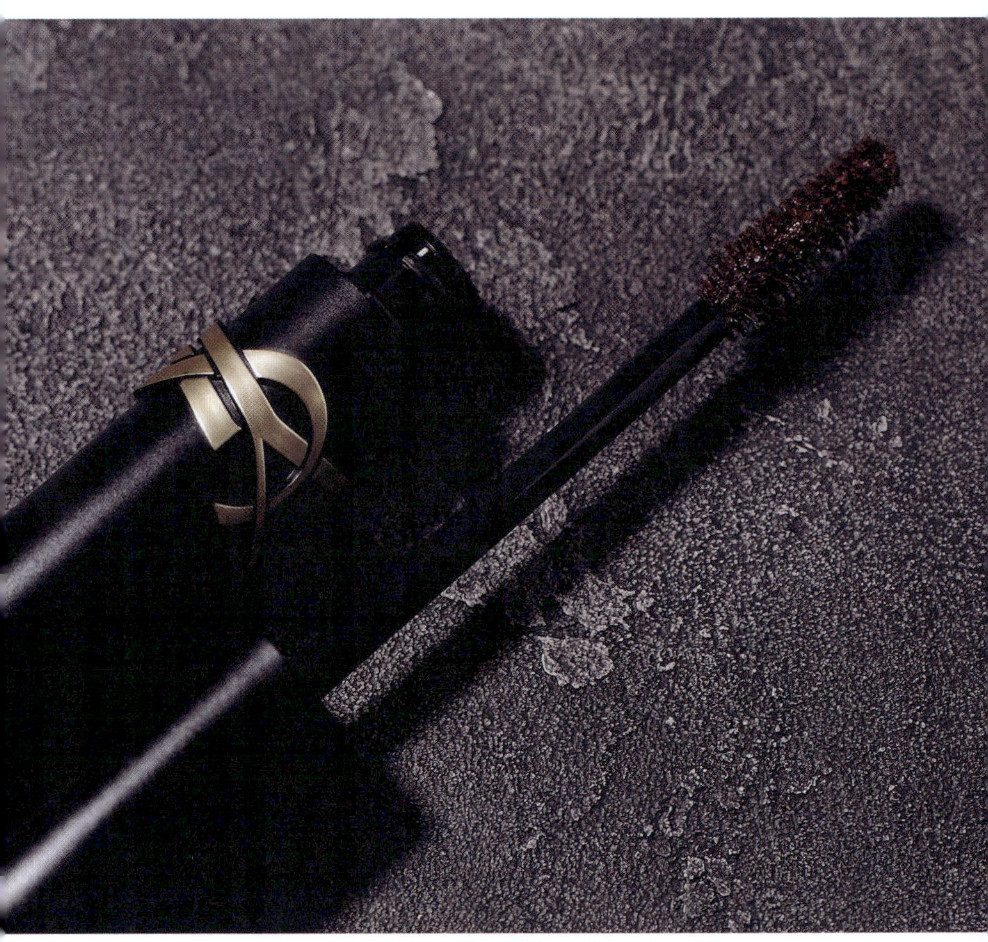

LASH CLASH EXTREME VOLUME MASCARA

The Lash Clash Extreme Volume Mascara is an Allure Magazine's "Best of Beauty" winner for 2023. This YSL Beauty mascara is top-notch for those who want length, volume, and all-around faux-looking lashes. The pigment on this mascara is nice and intense, coming in black, brown, or navy.

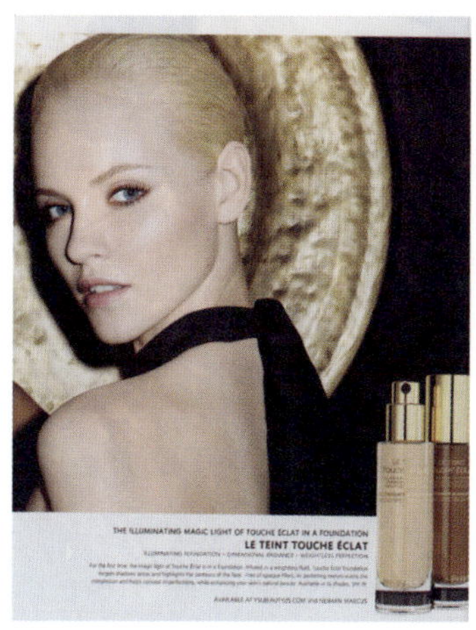

TOUCHE ÉCLAT ALL-OVER BRIGHTENING PEN

The Touche Éclat All-Over Brightening Pen is a famous YSL Beauty product that has been loved for years. The company describes it as a highlighting, concealing, and brightening pen. You can use it under the eyes to highlight the cheekbones and right above the brow for an all-over glow. Dab it all over any imperfection. It's like a magic wand for your complexion that comes in different shades for any skin tone. Once you start using this truly genius makeup product, you won't want to live without it.

VINYL CREAM LIP STAIN

The Vinyl Cream Lip Stain is a unique lip product that leaves a glowing stain on the lips. It has a high-impact color with intense pigment coverage, comes in six different colors, and offers up to 10 hours of long wear. The best colors are Rose Player, which is often sold out, and Burgundy Vibes, a deep fuchsia that harkens back to the colors that YSL Beauty originally produced. If you prefer neutral colors, try Nude Champion, the ideal shade of "barely-there" lip color.

ALL HOURS FOUNDATION

All Hours Foundation is a long-wearing formula that provides up to 24 hours of coverage. Its matte finish and full coverage hide a multitude of imperfections, leaving the skin radiantly smooth and even. It comes in a wide range of shades for any skin tone and has the added benefit of SPF 30 to protect the skin from the damaging rays of the sun. It can be used by anyone with any skin type, as it doesn't clog the pores or irritate acne-prone skin. All Hours Foundation is all you'll ever need for perfect coverage.

SKINCARE

PURE SHOTS PERFECT PLUMPER FACE CREAM

The Pure Shots Perfect Plumper Face Cream provides an instant glow, and over time, it will help to reduce signs of aging. Minimize the appearance of lines and wrinkles, dark spots, and dehydration in the skin by using this face cream twice a day. Orange blossom, a powerful antioxidant that can protect against the signs of aging, is one of its main ingredients.

PURE SHOTS LIGHT UP BRIGHTENING SERUM

Serums are concentrated versions of skincare that can work wonders for the skin. The Pure Shots Light Up Brightening Serum is specifically meant to get rid of dark spots, also known as age spots or sunspots, leaving the skin looking more even and much brighter.

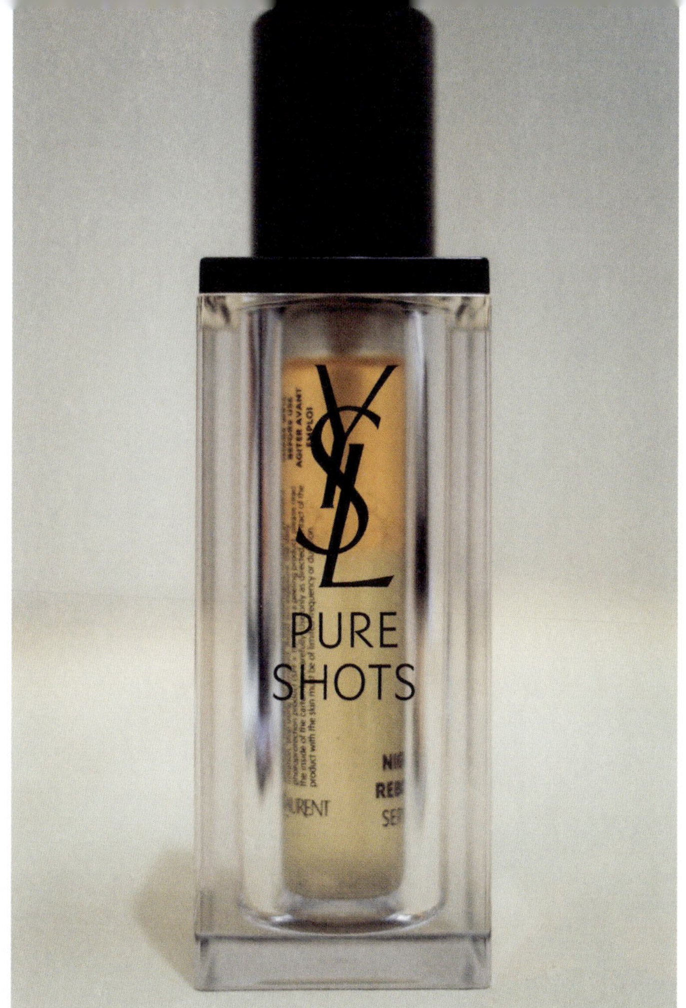

PURE SHOTS CLEAN REBOOT MOUSSE CLEANSER

The Pure Shots Clean Reboot Mousse Cleanser is a fantastic foaming face cleanser that removes makeup, oil, dirt, and debris from your skin. It is a twice-a-day cleanser that feels like it gets your skin squeaky clean without stripping the moisture barrier. With amino acids and jasmine flower extracts, your skin will feel pampered and ready to take in the rest of your skincare routine.

“YSL MAKEUP IS MY SECRET WEAPON FOR ACHIEVING THAT COVETED *‘FRENCH-GIRL CHIC’* LOOK. THEIR PRODUCTS GIVE ME THAT EFFORTLESS GLOW.”

Lily Collins

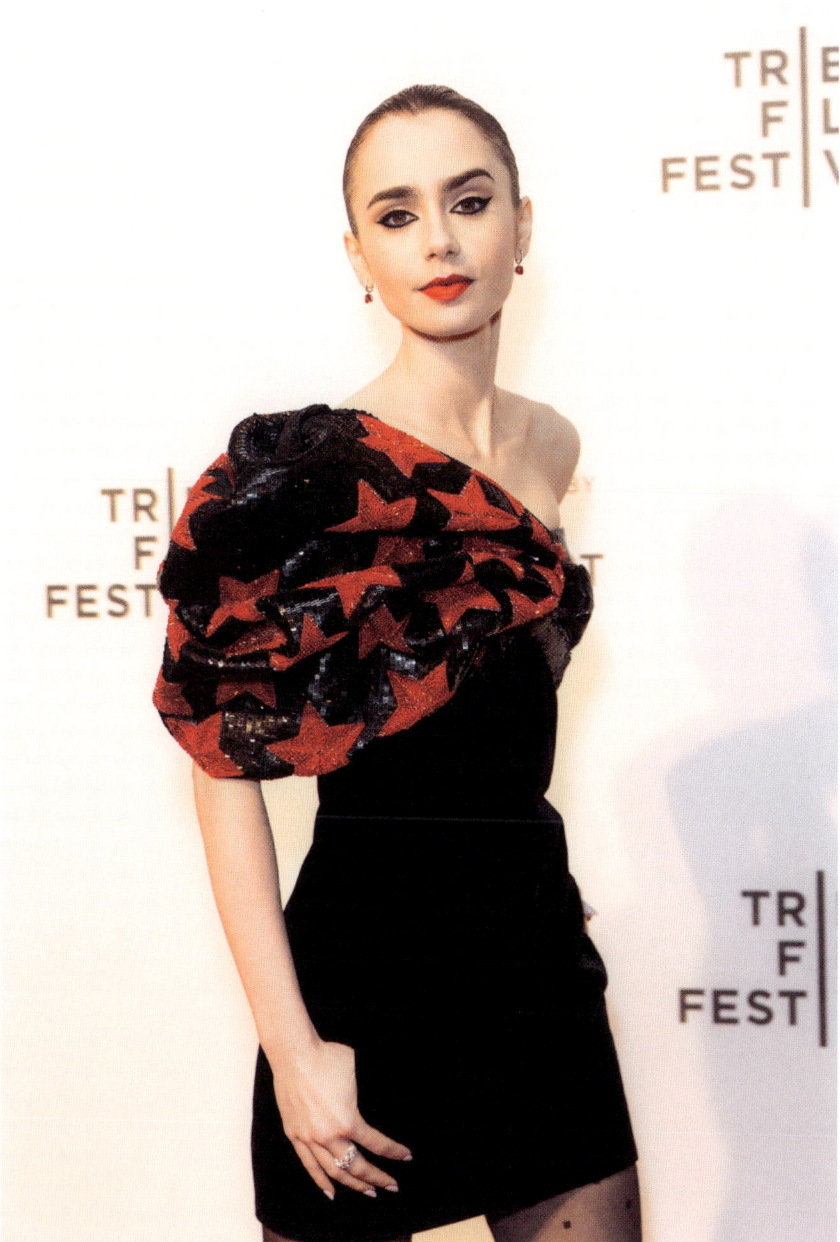

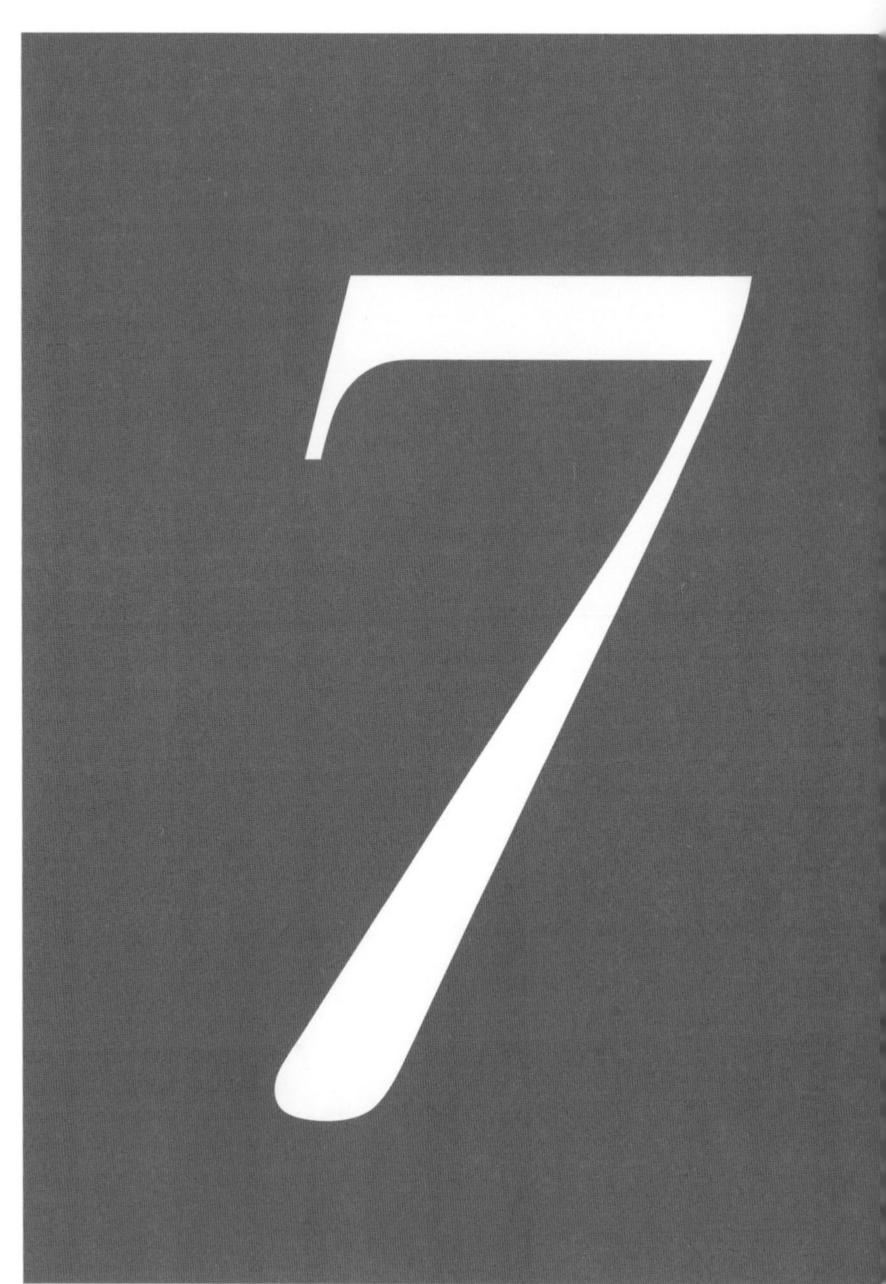

THE BEST of YSL FRAGRANCES

Fragrance

YVES SAINT LAURENT'S FORAY INTO FRAGRANCE started early in the fashion house's history, as Yves felt that fragrance was an important part of someone's allure. In 1964, he launched his first fragrance, called Y," in collaboration with the famed perfumer Jean Amic. Yves described it as "a lush, heavy, and languid perfume," and the fragrance itself was considered a green chypre, a strong citrusy but woody scent. The bottle was made to resemble the silhouette of a woman's frame. The "Y" was the subtle dip of her decolletage or neckline.

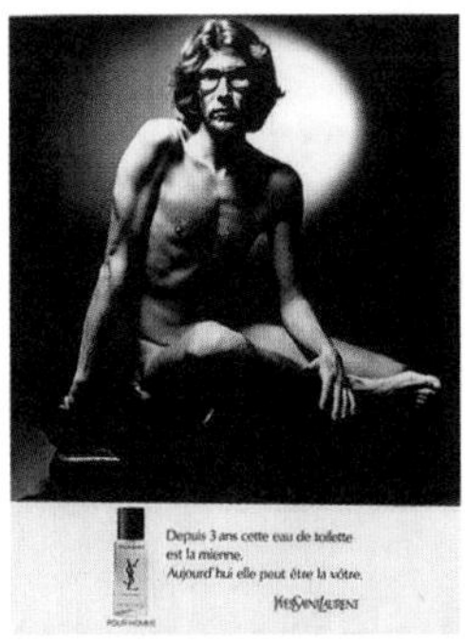

In 1971, Yves launched two other fragrances. The second fragrance for women was called Rive Gauche, after his successful ready-to-wear line. With notes of bergamot, peach, lemon, iris, and sandalwood, it was a unique and complex white floral fragrance. The next fragrance to come out that year was the first that YSL made for men. YSL Pour Homme was a classical masculine scent: woody, spicy, slightly lemony, and herbal. The most scandalous thing about the fragrance was the advertising for it, in which Yves himself posed nude. The fragrance was sophisticated, audacious, and very modern.

With these three products, the line was well on its way to creating a fragrance empire. Since the late '70s, YSL has produced quite a few additional scents. Let's look at some of the most memorable, starting with the magnificent Opium.

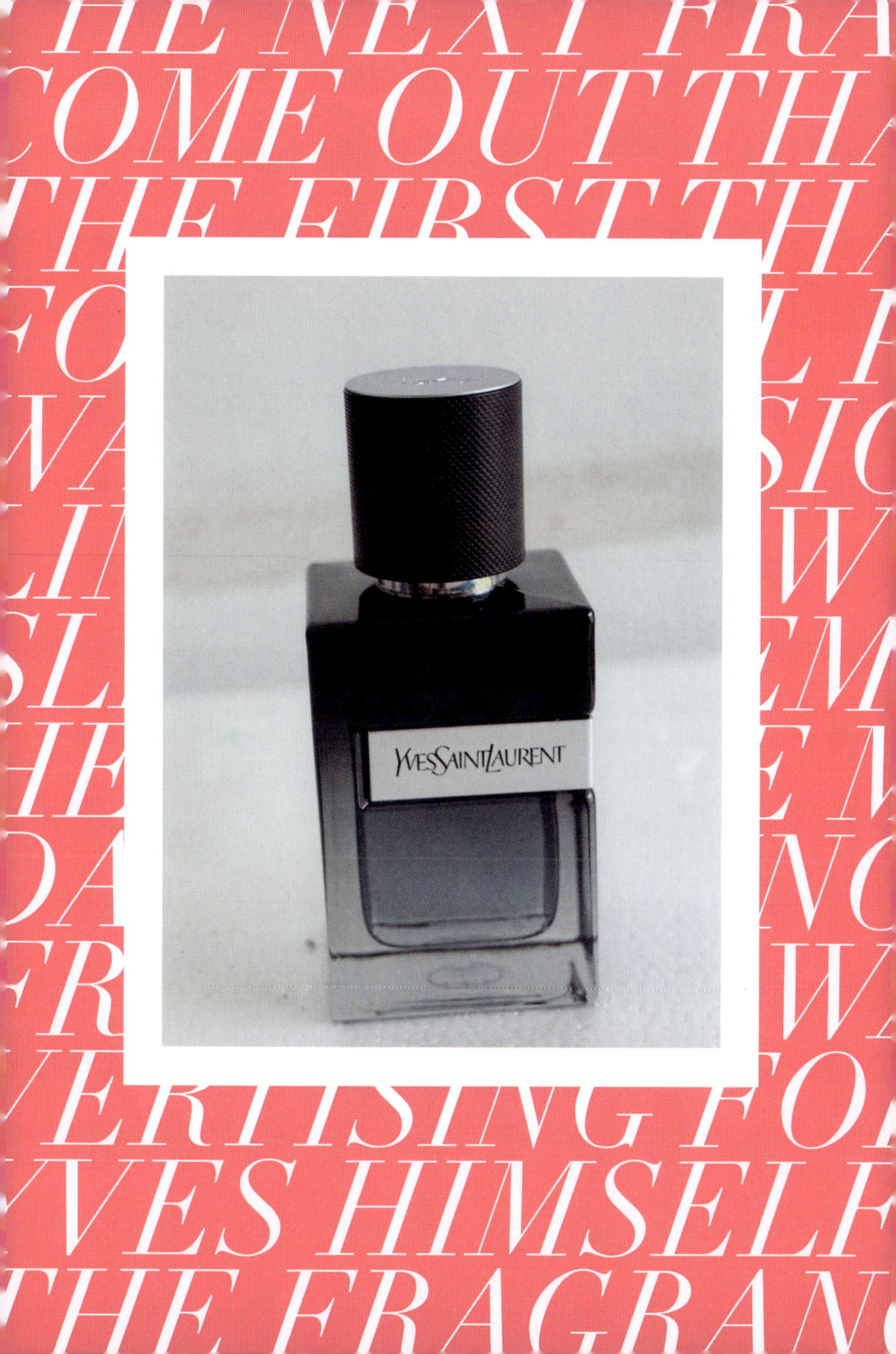
YVES SAINT LAURENT

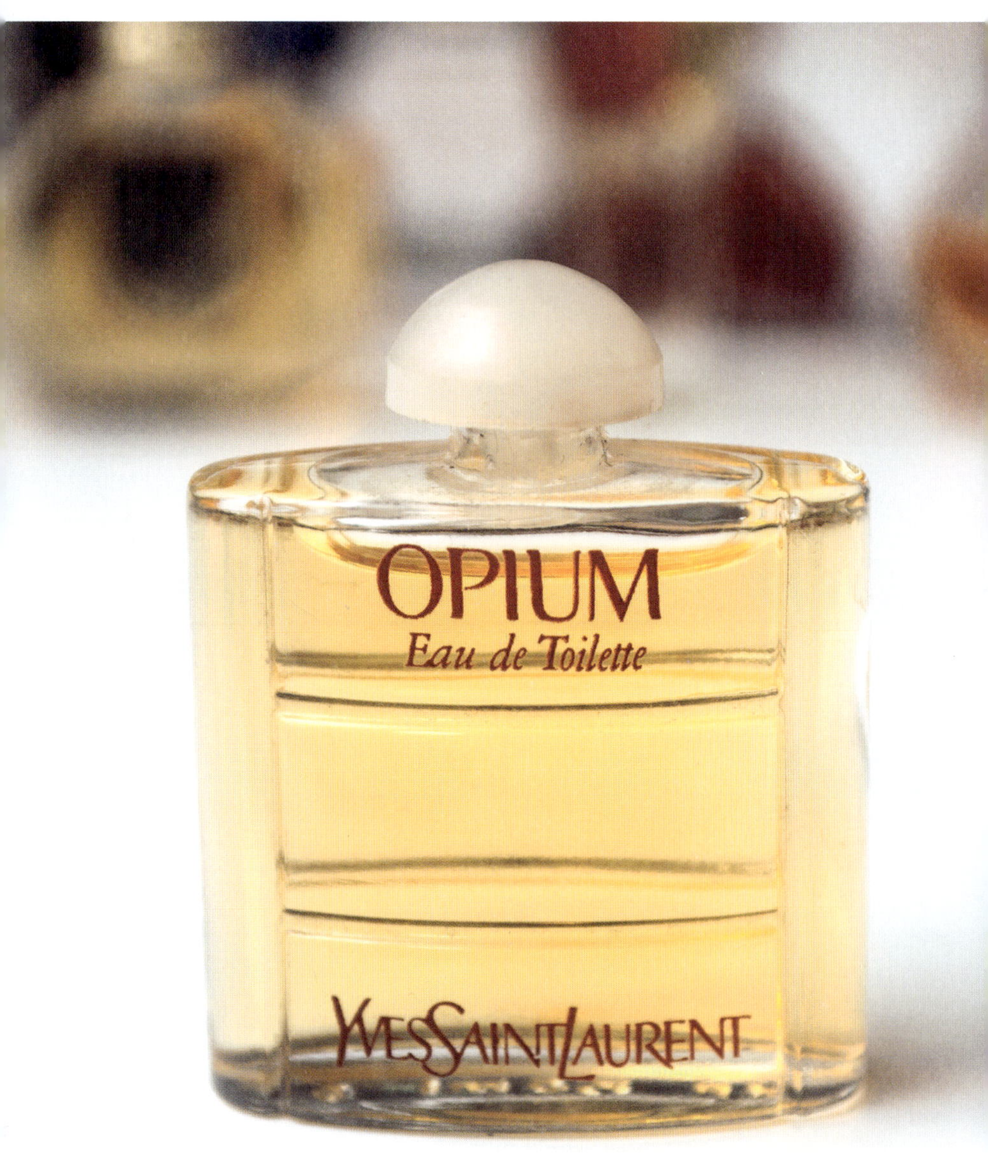
OPIUM
Eau de Toilette
YVES SAINT LAURENT

OPIUM

Opium was created by Jean-Louis Sieuzac and Jean Amic in 1977. It was a fantastic combination of amber and vanilla—sensuality, desire, and ecstasy in a bottle. The success of this fragrance was instant, with stores selling out and people stealing testers right off the display stands. In 2000, when the product was relaunched with a new model as the face, Sophie Dahl was naked in the ads. It was quite a scandal, and the ads only stayed around for five days before they were pulled from view. In addition, the name was considered problematic; it was seen as glorifying the drug culture, since opium is an illegal substance. Nevertheless, Opium continues to be one of the best-selling fragrances in the world, even to this day.

KOUROS

Described as the "scent of the gods," this is the second men's fragrance that YSL produced, launched in 1981. Its main notes are oak moss, patchouli, and musk. Classically male, the name represents the Ancient Greek sculptures of naked young men. YSL was always into pushing the boundaries of sensuality and sex in many of its fragrances.

YVRESSE

Originally called Champagne, this fragrance had to be renamed in 1993 after resistance from Champagne producers in France, who took YSL to court to force the name to be changed. The new name is a blend of the "Y" in Yves' name and the word ivresse, meaning "intoxication." Peach, nectarine, oak moss, and cinnamon give this fragrance a unique scent that blends differently on each person's skin. You can't find it on the YSL Beauty website, but it is still sold by Harrods in Britain, both in-store and online.

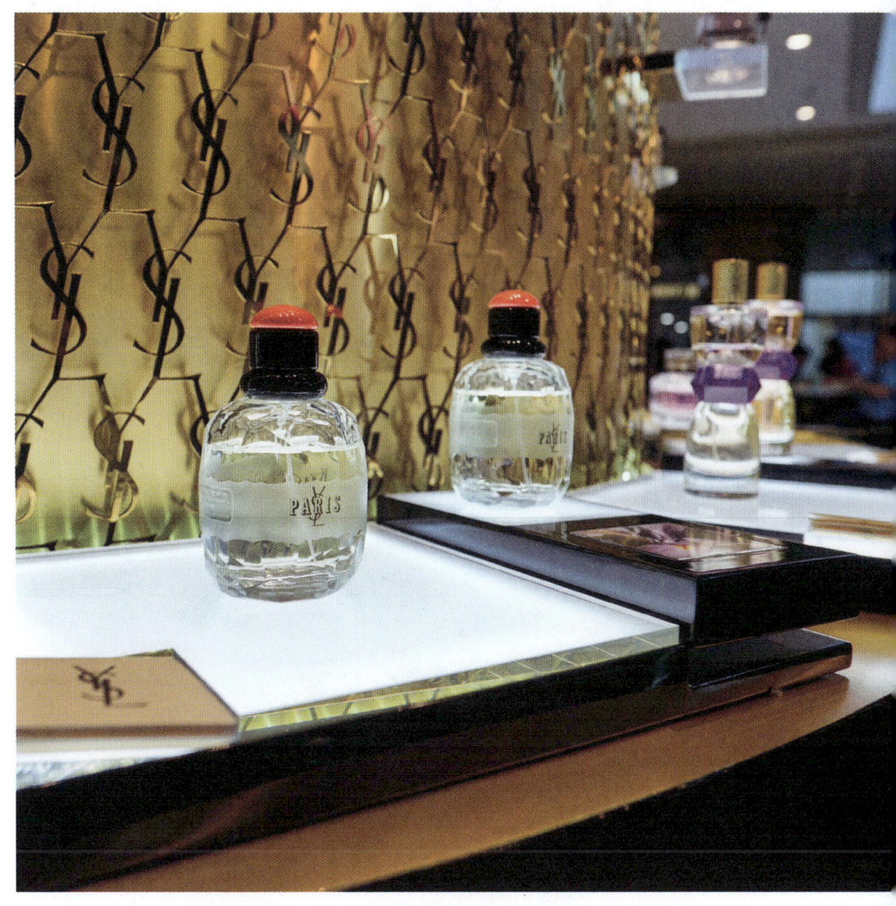

PARIS

The year 1983 brought about a fresh new fragrance for YSL. It was made by perfumer Sophia Grojsman. By naming it Paris, Yves wanted to pay tribute to the city that had given him so much and in which he had started his famous fashion house. The scent itself came in a pretty beveled bottle with a peach-colored cap. The notes in it were sparkling and sweet with mimosa, orange blossom, vanilla, rose, and sandalwood. Overall, this powdery, floral fragrance is still quite popular today.

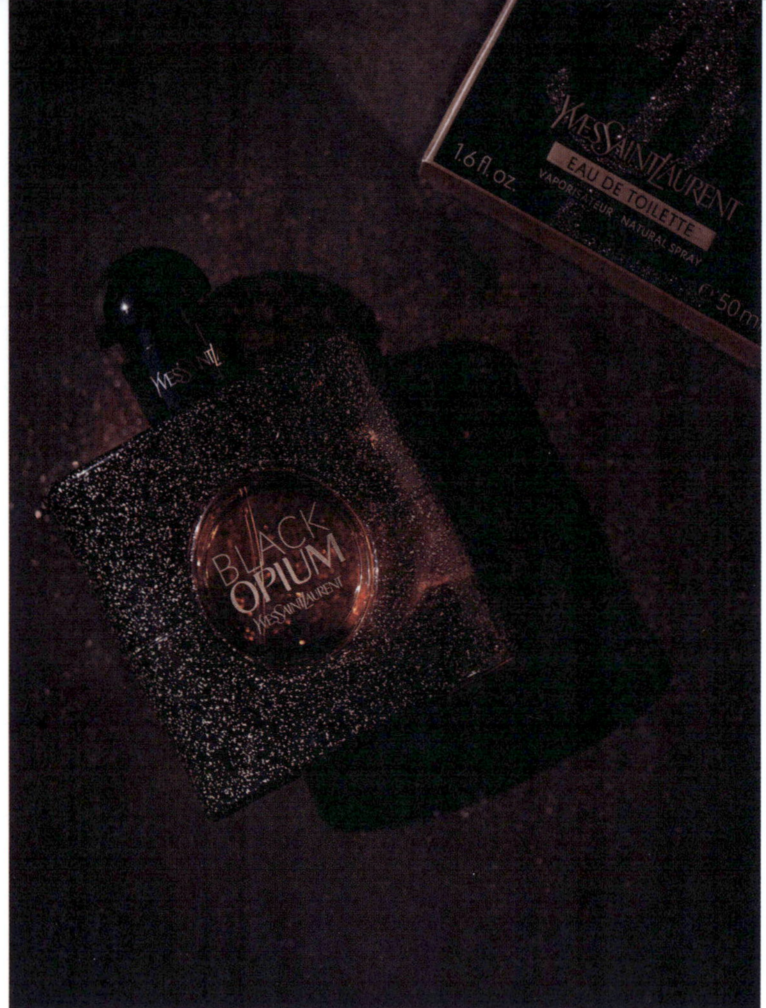

BLACK OPIUM

In September 2014, four master perfumers were tasked with coming up with a new Opium. Black Opium was born through the work of Olivier Cresp, Nathalie Lorson, Honorine Blanc, and Marie Salamagne. It's an original scent with notes of black coffee, vanilla, and different white floral accords. The bottle is eye-catching, sparkling black with a pink center that says "Black Opium." This fragrance had kind of a rock n' roll edge to its look to celebrate the modern woman, who is fearless and bold. The year after this fragrance was created, it won the prestigious Fragrance Foundation Award for "Best New Fragrance."

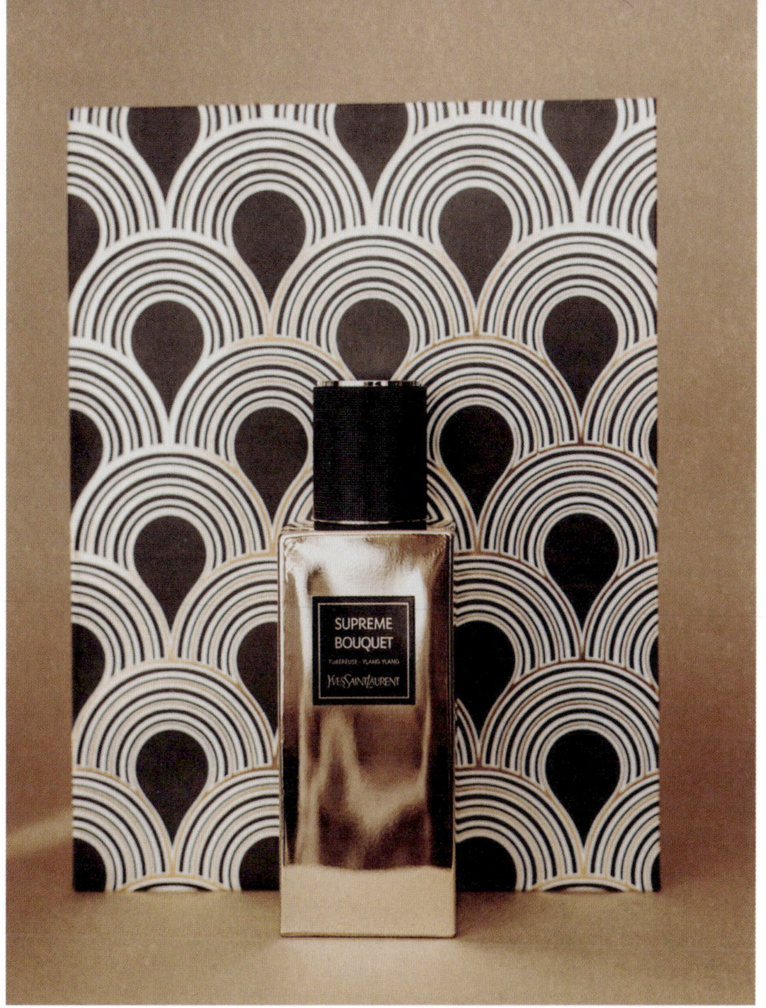

THE AMBREE COLLECTION

In 2009, the Ambree Collection was produced. This was a collection of four different fragrances: Supreme Bouquet, Noble Leather, Majestic Rose, and Splendid Wood. These fragrances are supposed to have been inspired by different rooms in a grand palace in the Middle East. The name of each one pretty much describes exactly what it smells like, so there's not a lot of mystery there.

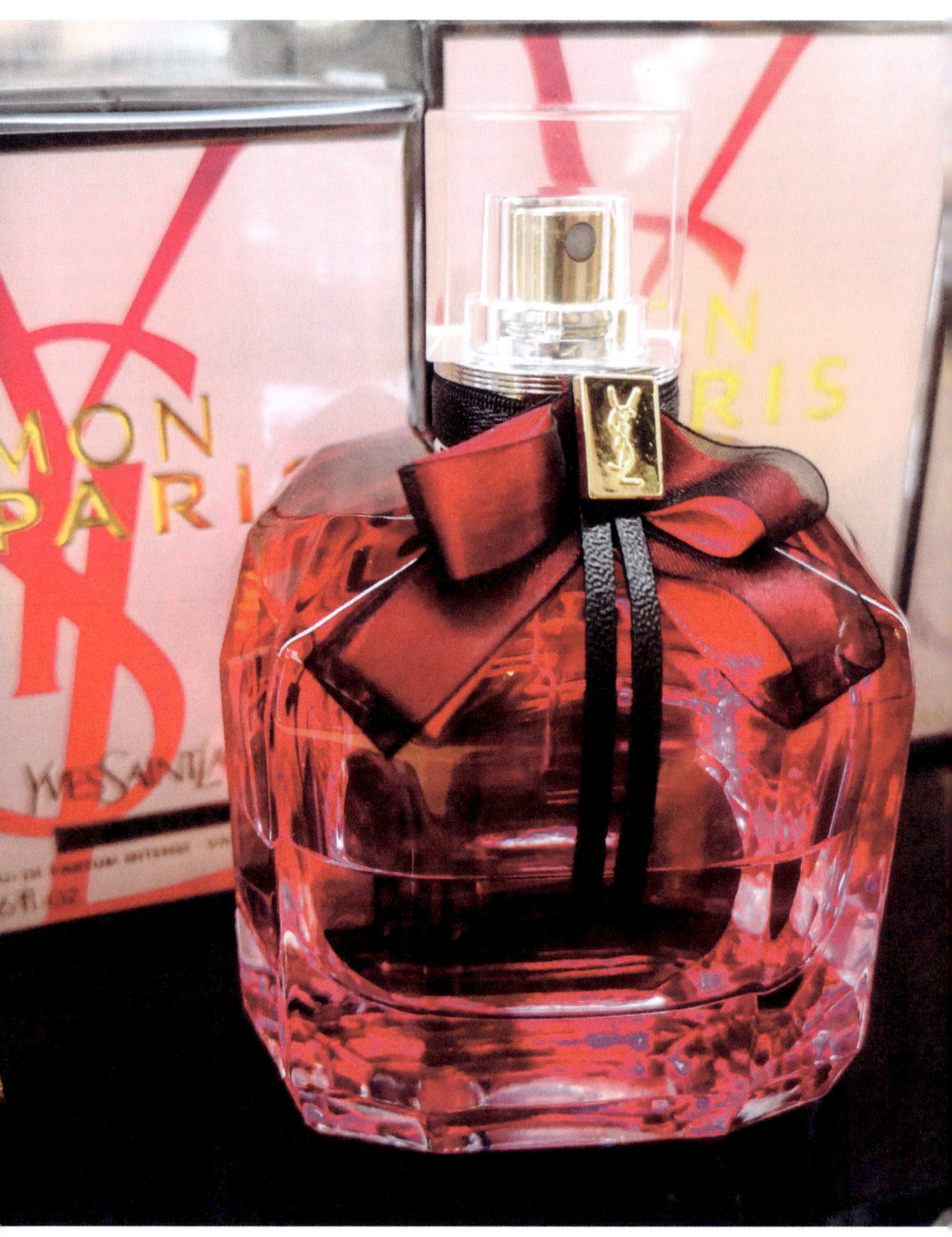
MON

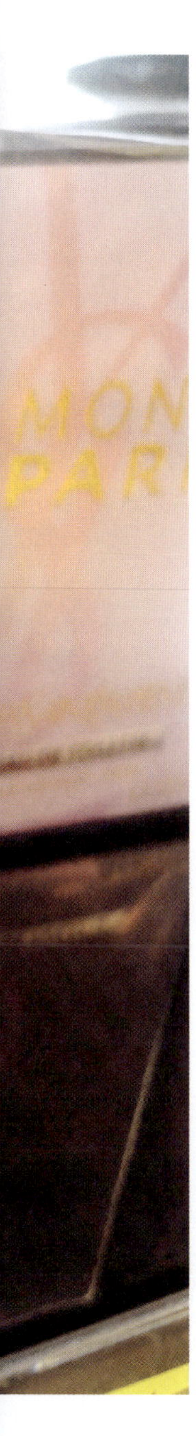

MON PARIS

Mon Paris was launched in 2016 with a pretty, clear bottle that showed off the violet-colored fragrance within. The notes are truly original, with YSL describing this fragrance as the first white chypre. It is fruity and sweet, with strawberry, orange, jasmine, and white musk layered throughout the notes, and it has a dark chypre base. An interesting fragrance that feels both sexy and alive, it is still one of their best-sellers today.

LIBRE

Libre is one of YSL's newest fragrances, joining the YSL Beauty family in 2019. You may have seen the commercials starring pop sensation Dua Lipa. One of its taglines is "We live life by our own rules." The Latin word libre means the state of being free. This fragrance has a white floral scent with citrus and lavender undertones in the middle notes. The base is a little powdery and sweet, with some vanilla and musk to balance it all out. Anne Flipo and Carlos Benaim were the perfumers who created this one.

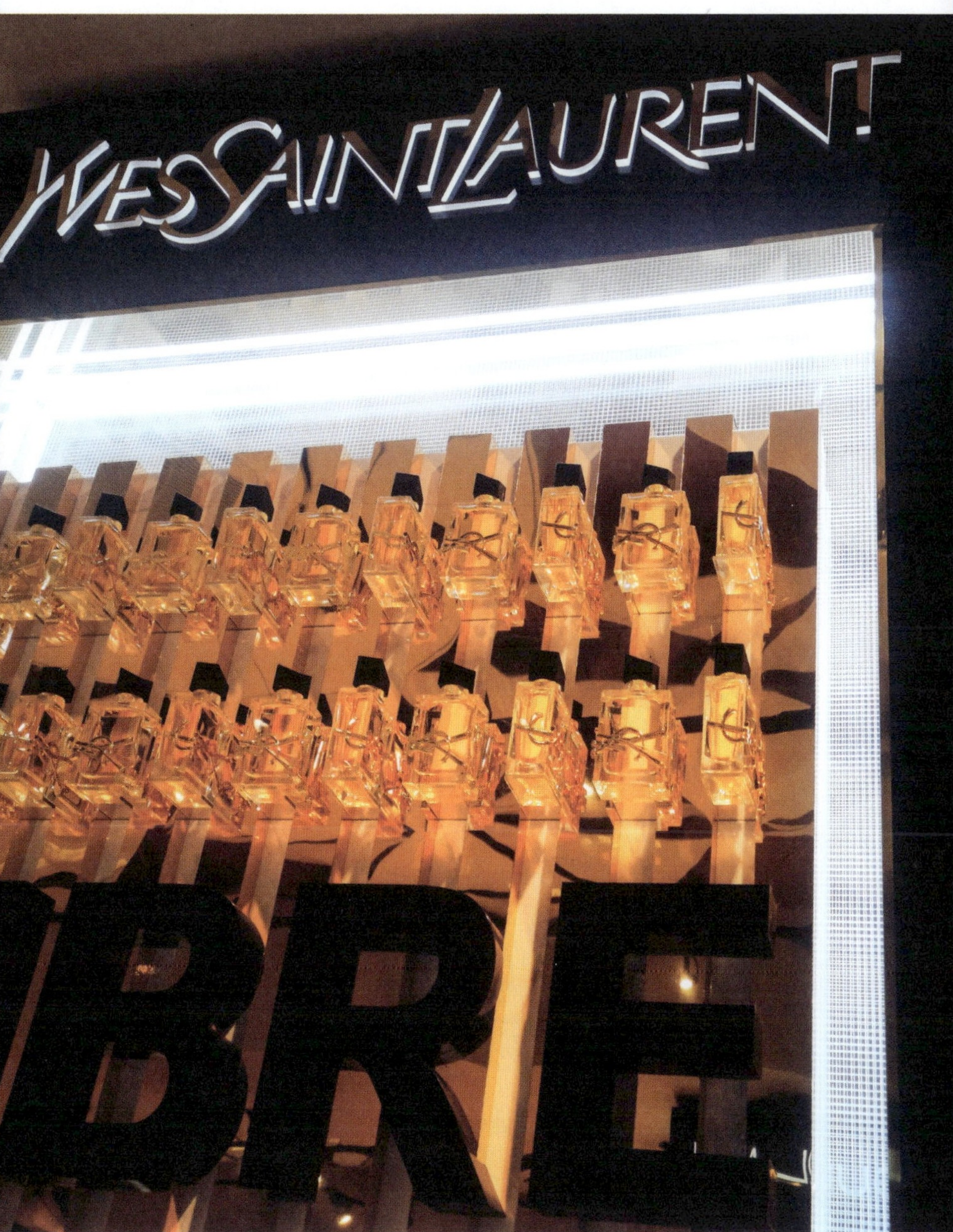
YVES SAINT LAURENT
BRE

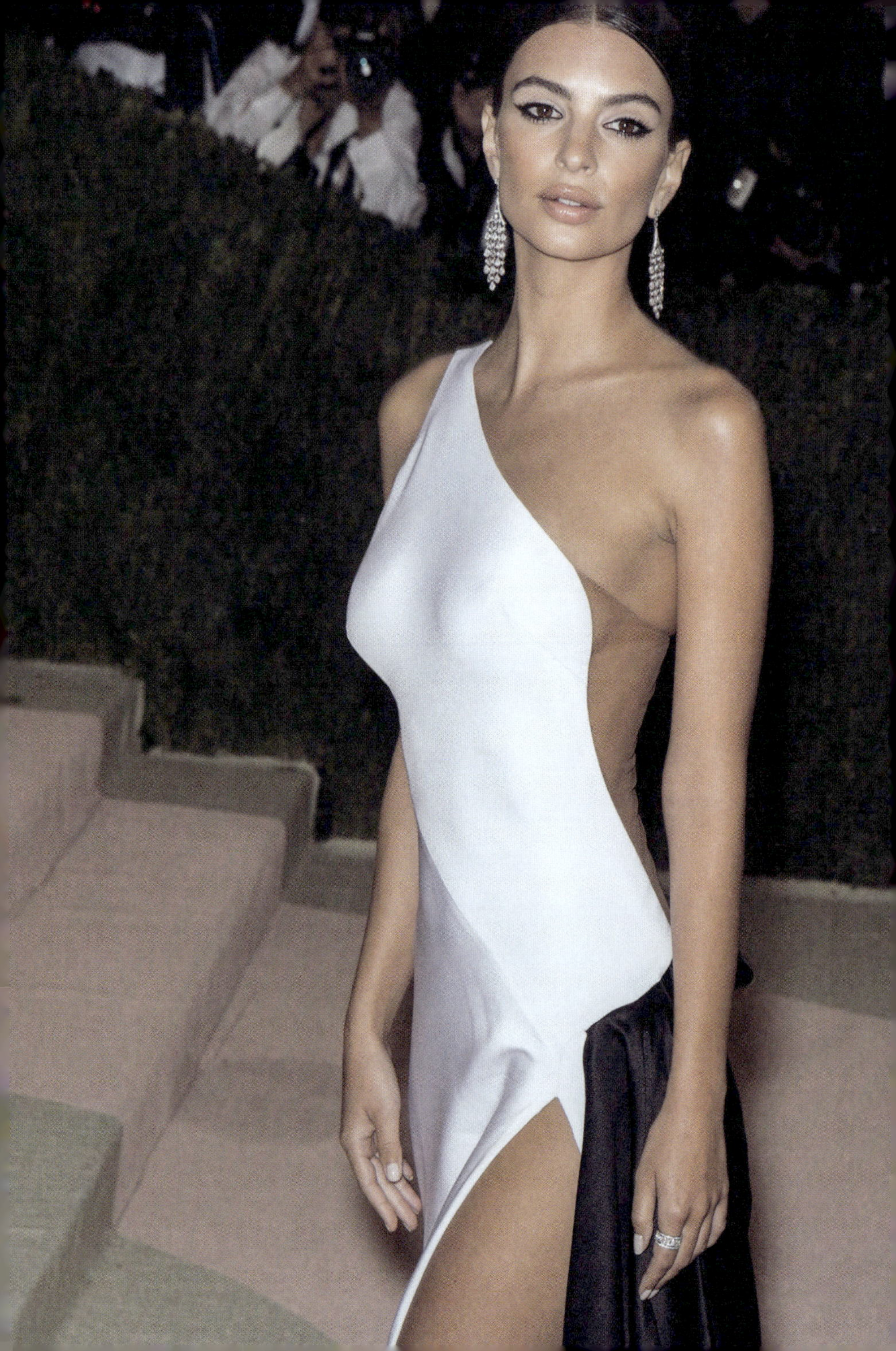

“YSL BLACK OPIUM IS MY ABSOLUTE FAVORITE. *IT'S SEXY AND INTOXICATING* WITHOUT BEING OVER-POWERING.”

Emily Ratajkowski

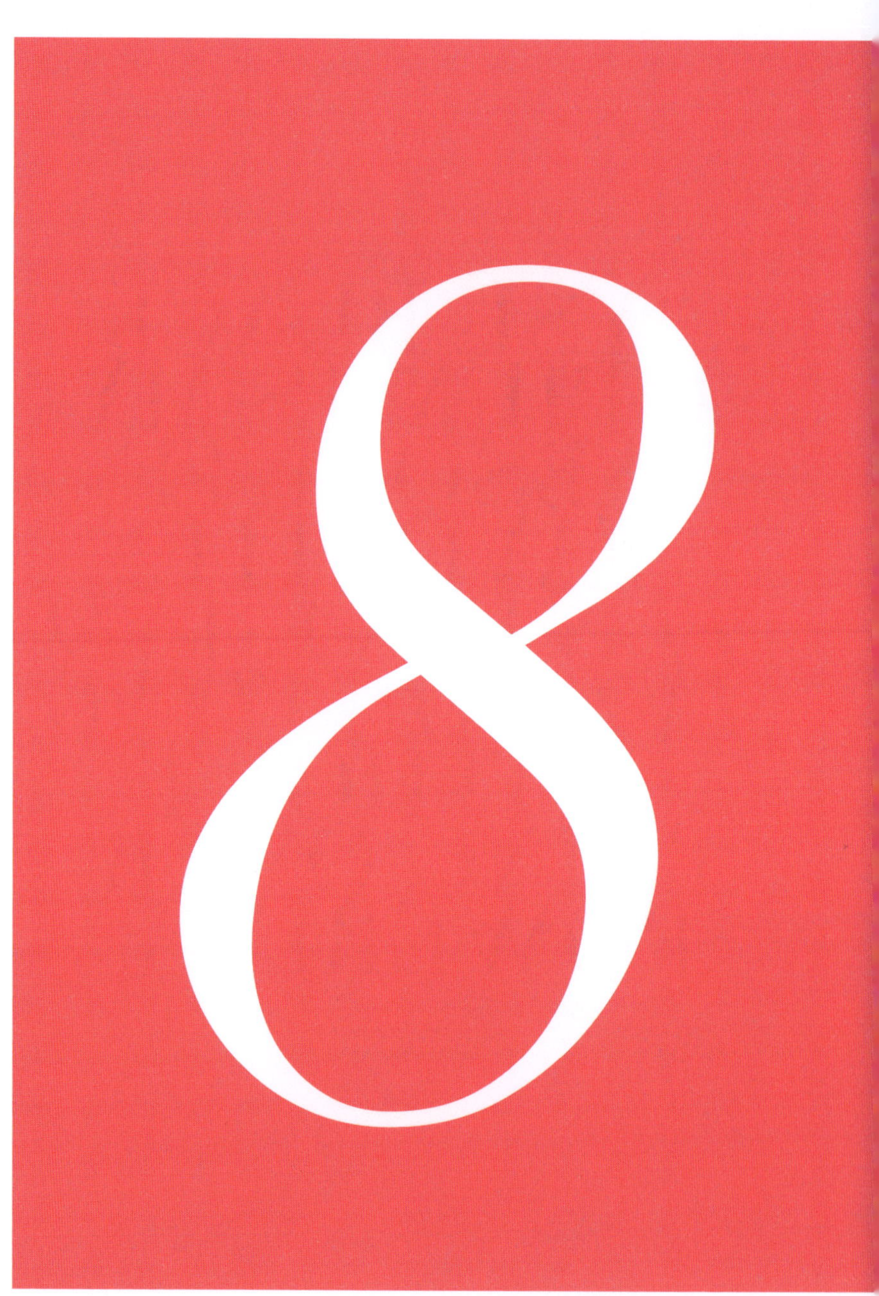

YSL'S COOLEST AMBASSADORS

Famous Models

MODELS AND AMBASSADORS have always been an important part of any fashion house. This is especially true for YSL, which—along with its couture and ready-to-wear lines, accessories, and beauty products—has needed to have some truly stand-out people to represent it.

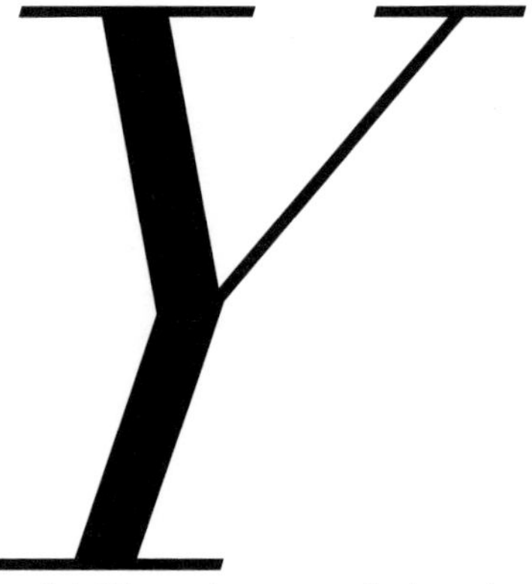

ves Saint Laurent was an early champion of diversity. His was the first luxury fashion house to use African American models in his runway shows, with Amalia Vairelli, Mounia Orosemane, and Katoucha Niane being some of his favorite models who appeared in many of his shows over the years.

He loved to design with a live fashion model next to him. Yves once said, “When I see a fashion model, I know what I'm going to design for her. It's like love at first sight. I fall in love.” Laetitia Casta was one of those with whom he fell in love. She was a famous model who met Yves in 1996 and quickly became one of his favorites. Her figure was curvier than that of most of the runway models, but Yves didn't care. He called her his “bird of paradise.” For the 2000 Spring/Summer collection, he designed for her a dress made up of lots of feathers from an exotic bird.

Here are some of the newest ambassadors for YSL. They are some of the hottest young stars today.

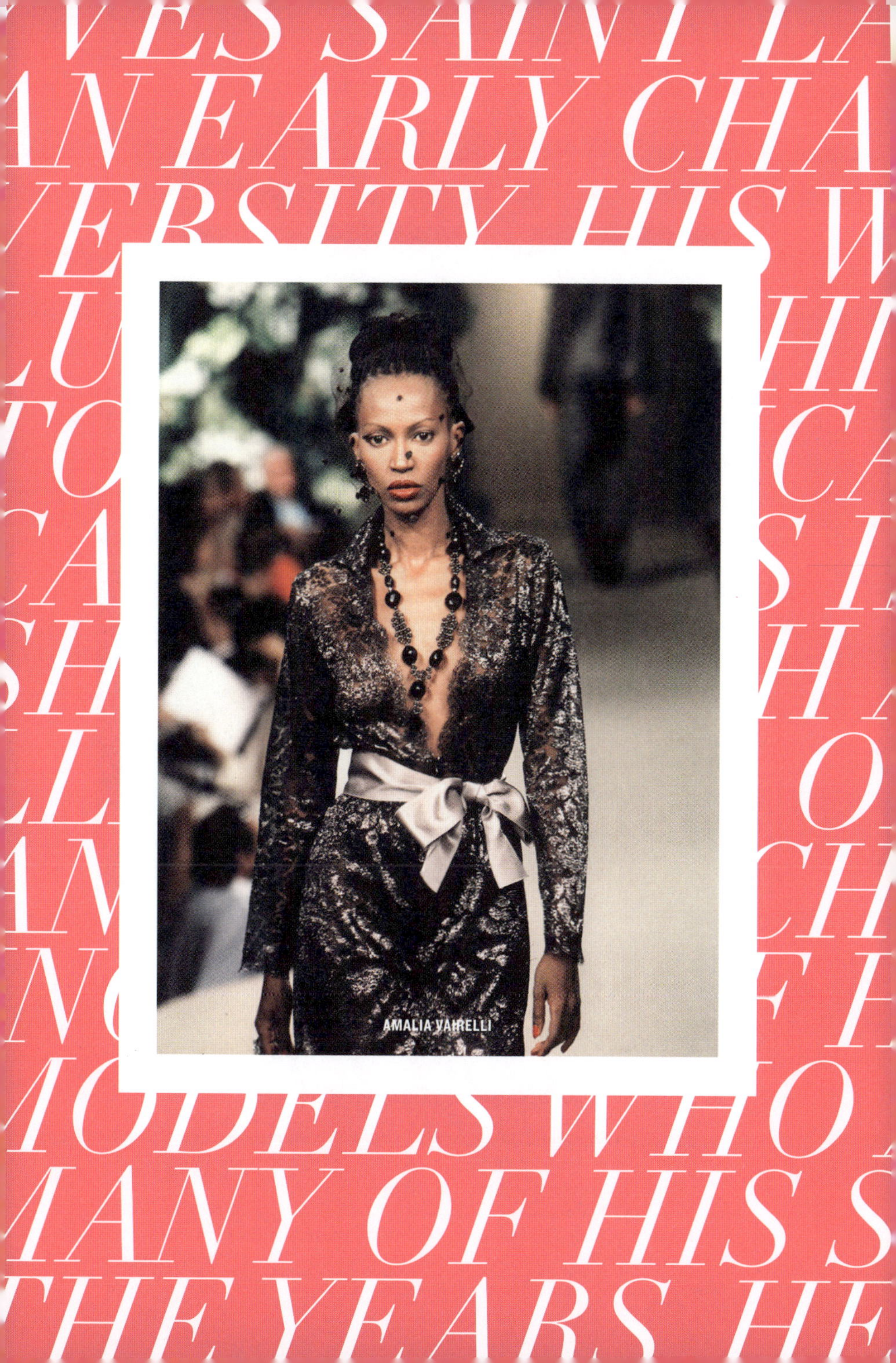

AMALIA VAIRELLI

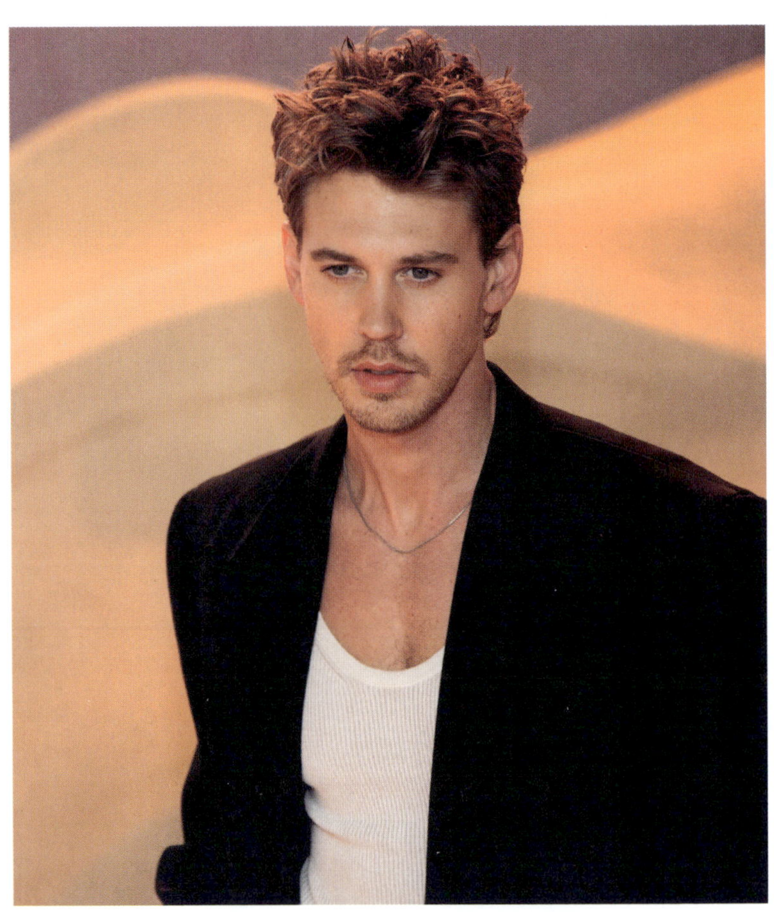

AUSTIN *BUTLER*

Actor Austin Butler is the face of YSL's men's fragrances—specifically, he features in the ads for MYSLF. The actor said that before he accepted the modeling role for YSL, he researched who Yves Saint Laurent was and discovered that Yves was a true rebel, breaking through labels to make his way into fashion history.

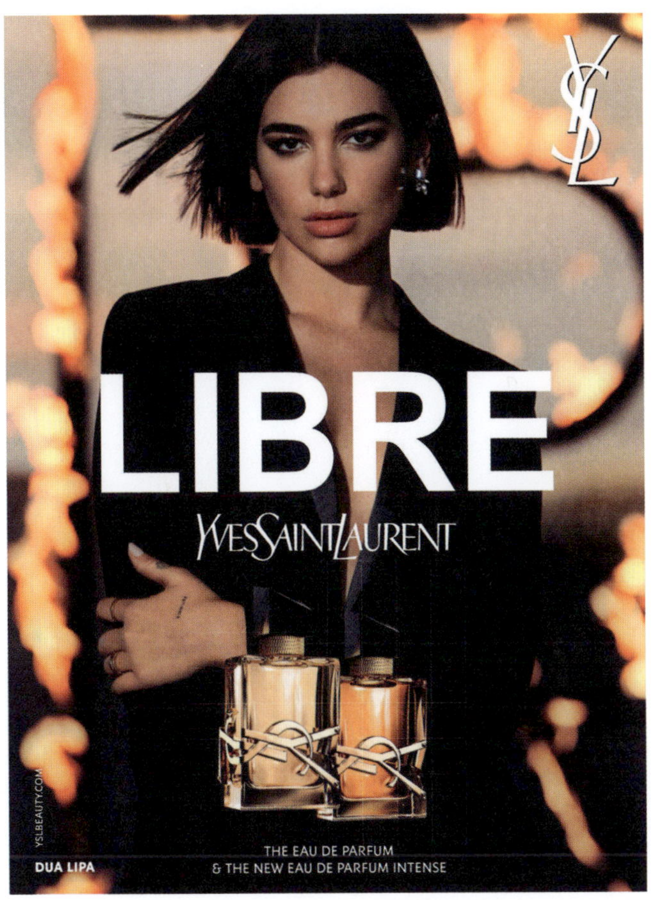

DUA *LIPA*

Pop princess Dua Lipa was named one of YSL Beauty's Global Ambassadors. She has been seen in the Libre fragrance ads since 2019, and now she also stars in the ads for some of the beauty products. She has helped to promote the Loveshine lipstick line, which has a few different lip products, including a lip oil stick.

ROSÉ

K-Pop group Blackpink counts Rosé as one of their members, and she has been an ambassador for YSL for several years. She loves the elegant and classic looks that YSL has, so she is often seen wearing the clothing at red carpet events. Rosé has been in ads for YSL clothing since 2020. She is featured in gorgeous black and white ads that show off not only the clothes but also some of the accessories, like the Solferino handbag.

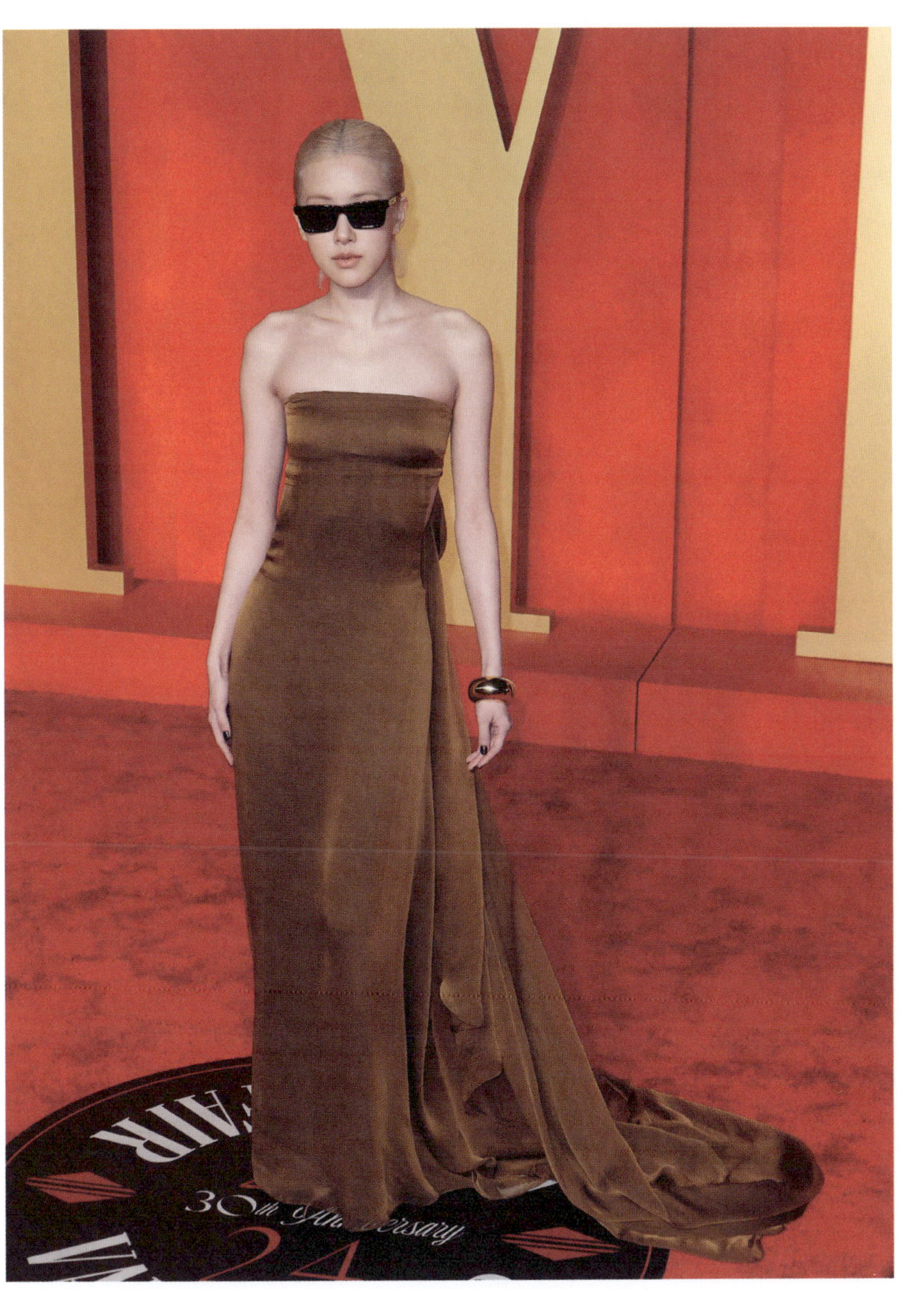

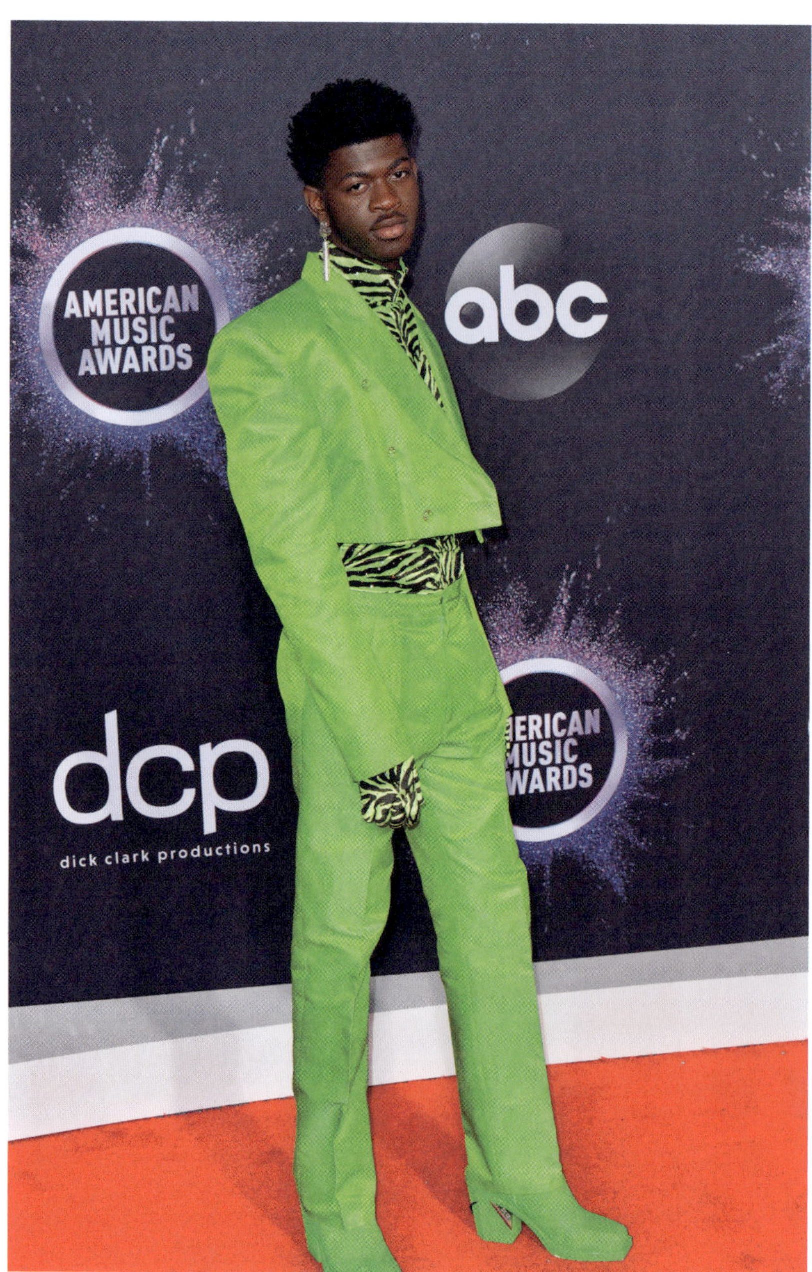
AMERICAN
MUSIC
AWARDS
abc
dcp
dick clark productions

LIL NAS *X*

Rapper and activist Lil Nas X is a force to be reckoned with, which is why he was tapped to be a beauty ambassador for the brand in 2023. He even wore YSL makeup on the red carpet of the Met Gala in 2022. Experimenting with color and challenging traditional masculinity makes him the ideal ambassador for a forward-thinking company such as YSL.

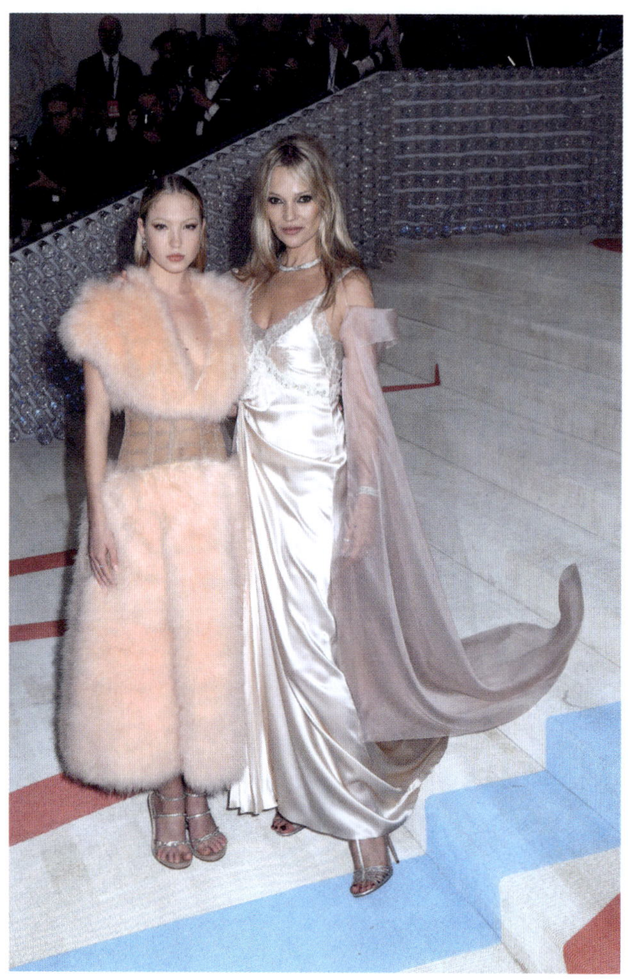

LILA *MOSS*

Model Lila Moss comes by her profession honestly—her mom is Kate Moss, the famous '90s supermodel. In 2022, Lila became one of YSL Beauty's Global Ambassadors. Her favorite lipstick is Candy Glaze, which she has mentioned many times in interviews. She appeared in Korean Vogue, photographed by Anthony Vaccarello, posing in a café in Paris and looking very chic in YSL couture.

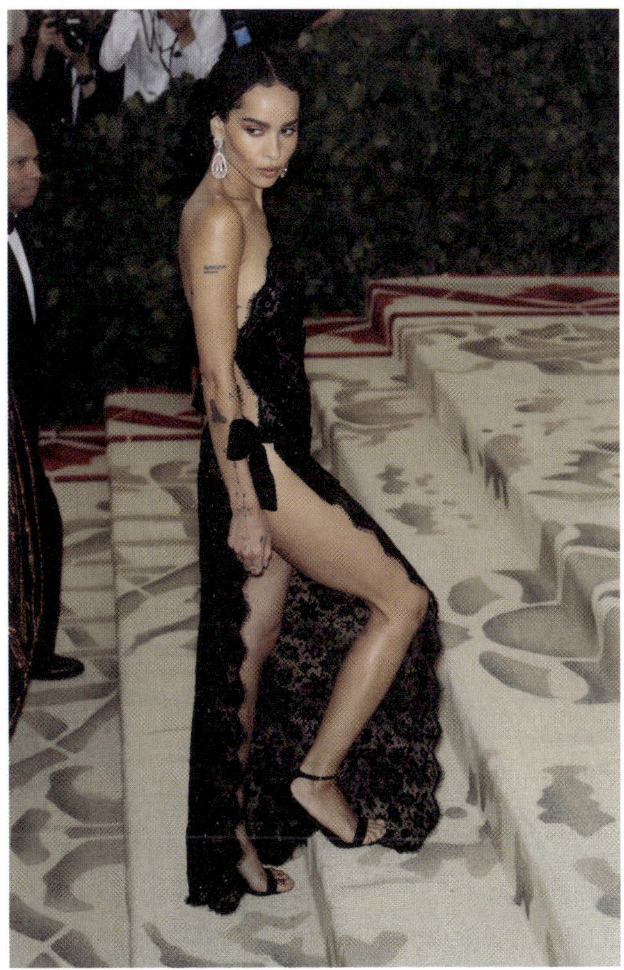

ZOË *KRAVITZ*

Actress Zoë Kravitz has starred in many campaigns for YSL, including some for Black Opium, handbags, and different clothing lines. As one of the best ambassadors for YSL, she stands out on red carpets and in anything she wears for the brand. Her edgy style provides the ideal look that helps maintain YSL's reputation as a modern luxury fashion house.

“YVES SAINT LAURENT WAS A GENIUS *AND A VISIONARY WHO FOREVER CHANGED THE LANDSCAPE OF FASHION.*”

Naomi Campbell

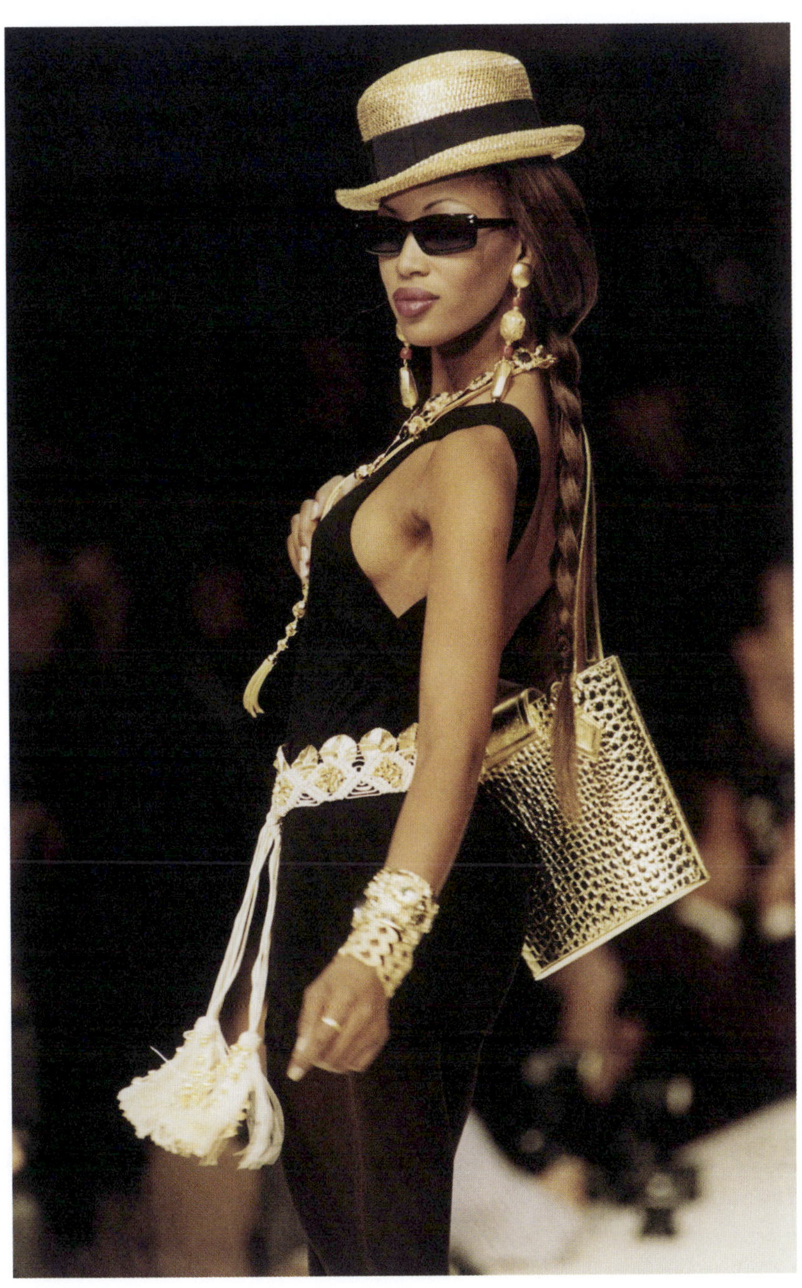

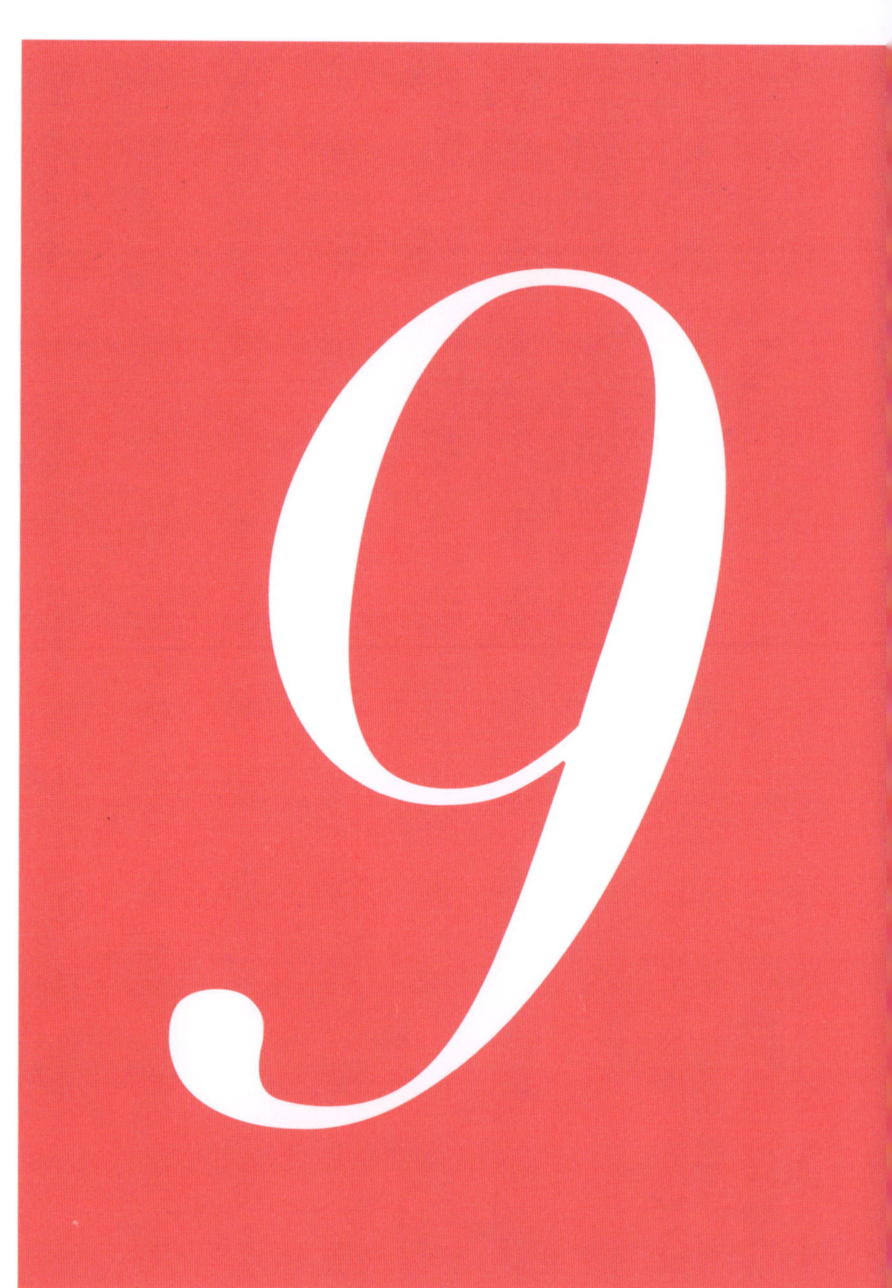

YSL FOR EVENTS *and* AWARD SHOWS

Celebrities

TODAY, AS IN DECADES PAST, CELEBRITIES OFTEN SHOW UP for red carpet events wearing Yves Saint Laurent. There have been some outstanding looks over the years, worn by royalty, rock stars, and actors, that have been a part of fashion history. From the Le Smoking tuxedo jacket to YSL's Safari Jacket and everything in between, when a famous person wears YSL, it gets noticed. Here are some major celebrities who have rocked YSL couture and ready-to-wear lines on the red carpet.

ANGELINA JOLIE

This beautiful actress has long been a fan of Yves Saint Laurent. One of her most memorable looks was a take on menswear for the 2014 BAFTA Awards where she wore an undone version of the Le Smoking jacket with a partially unbuttoned white blouse, untied bowtie, and skinny tuxedo pants. The whole look was edgy, glam, cool, and completely sophisticated. A skinny black belt and pointy-toed pumps completed the style.

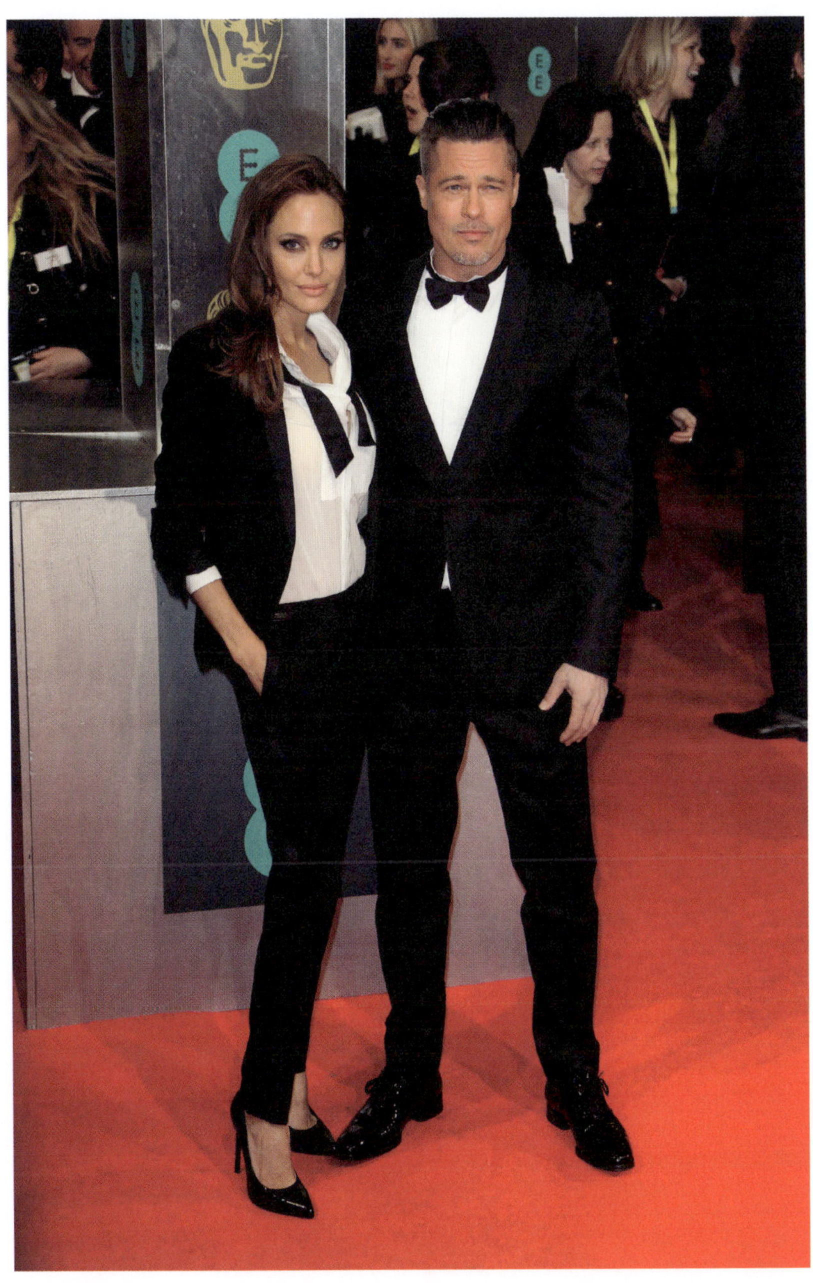

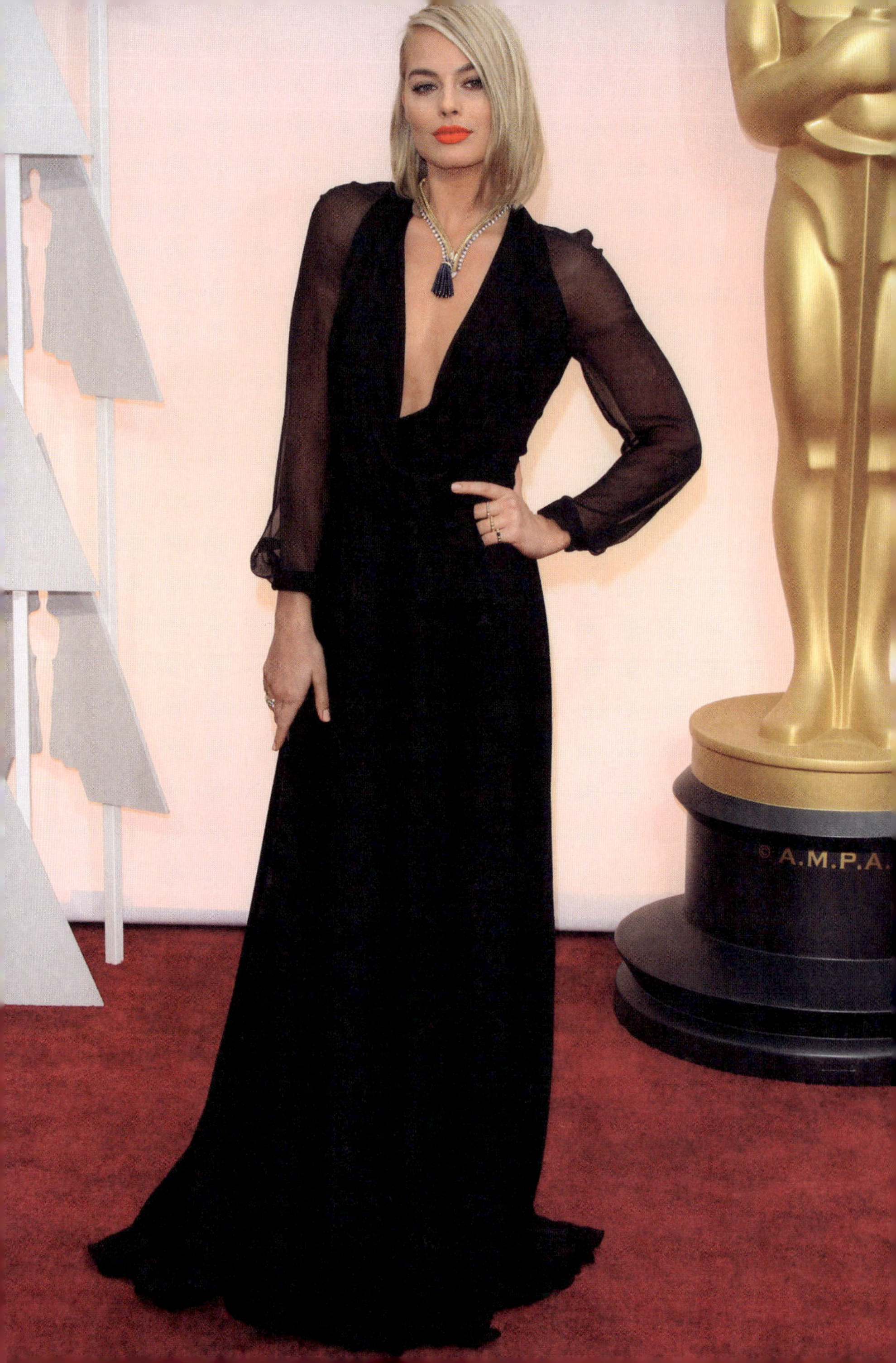
© A.M.P.A.

MARGOT ROBBIE

The outstanding Margo Robbie of Barbie is a good friend to YSL, regularly showing up on the red carpet in the couture styles. One of her most noteworthy looks was at the Academy Awards in 2015 where she wore a floor-length sheer black gown that had a deep V-neck and flowy sleeves. The look was very old Hollywood glam on one of the hottest stars on the planet.

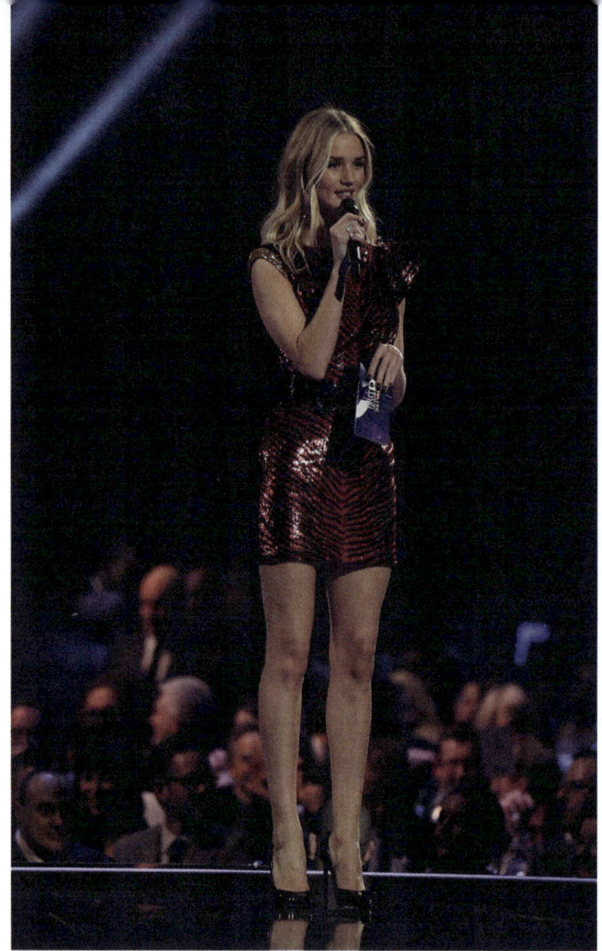

ROSIE HUNTINGTON-WHITELEY

Model Rosie Huntington-Whiteley was another standout on the red carpet in 2014. Attending the Brit Awards, she wore a sparkling red zebra print YSL minidress with a black bow around her waist. It was a fun look that was a bit of a throwback to the '80s. She looked gorgeous and modern in this dress.

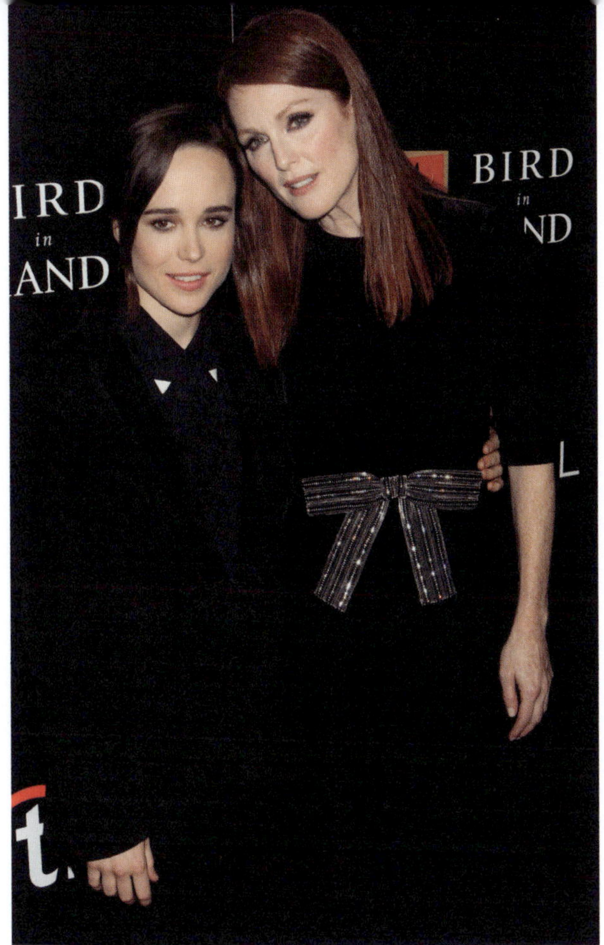

JULIANNE MOORE

Julianne Moore has been a familiar face on the red carpet for years. The effortless way this actress wears clothes is simply breathtaking. One of her best YSL looks was in 2015 at the art premiere of the Museum of Modern Art in New York City. She wore a floor-length black velvet dress with a silver sequined bow in the front. The most interesting aspect of this dress is that it had been a miniskirt when it was shown on the runway for Fall 2015. Hedi Slimane lengthened it just for Julianne to wear, making it dressier and even more elegant.

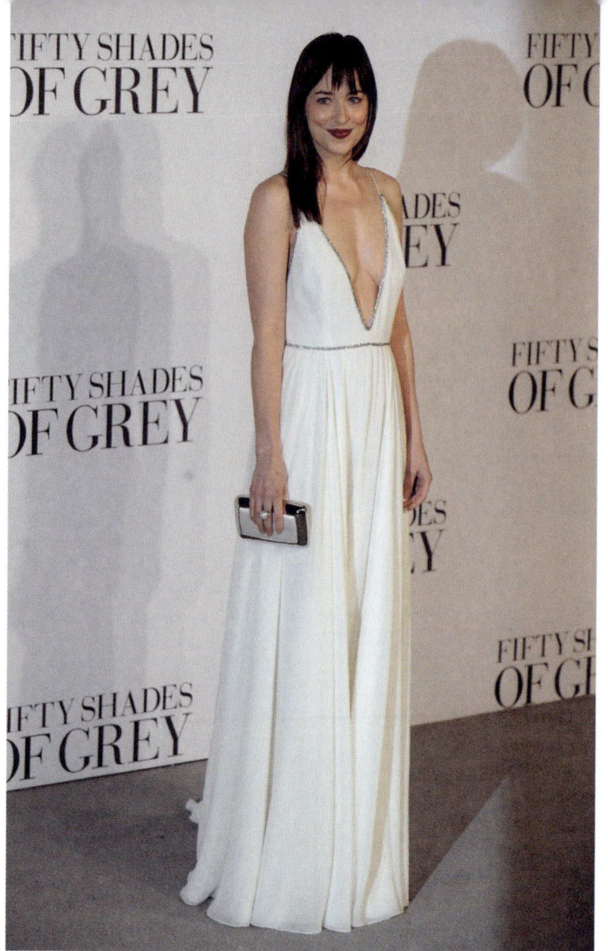

DAKOTA JOHNSON

Eternal "It Girl" and actress Dakota Johnson knows what she looks great in, and YSL is clearly one of the fashion houses that is always ready to dress this beauty. In 2015, for the London premiere of her movie Fifty Shades of Grey, she wore the most goddess-looking gown in ethereal white. The gown went all the way down to the floor and had an elegant train, a plunging deep V neckline, and tiny delicate straps. The rhinestone detailing had crystals surrounding the neckline and around the waist. She was a walking angel.

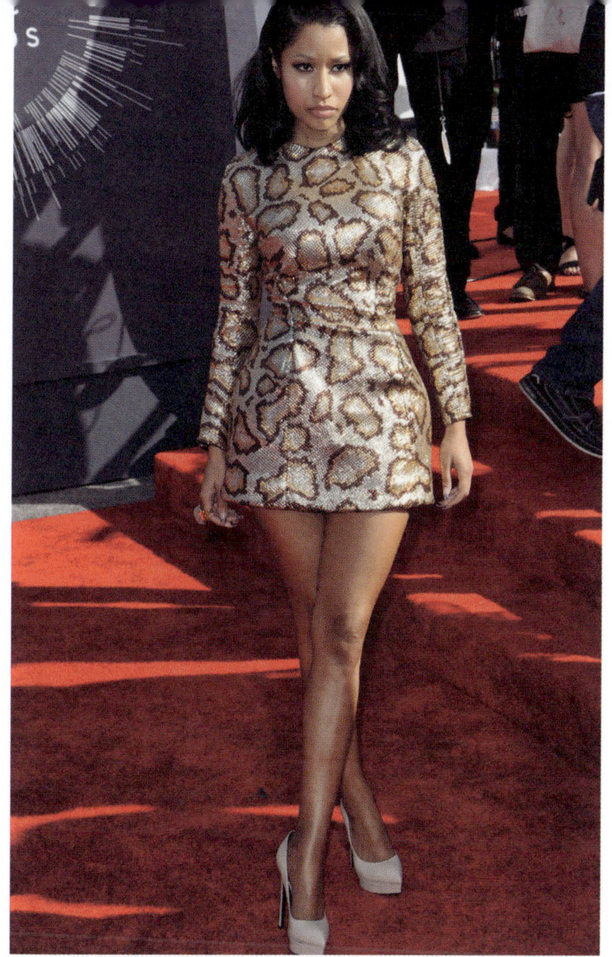

NICKI MINAJ

She performed alone with 'Anaconda' and together with Usher with 'She Came to Give It to You' at the MTV VMA 2014. On the red carpet, Nicki Minaj wore a gold shimmering dress with a high hemline balanced out with long sleeves. The dress was taken directly from the Fall 2014 fashion show, but Minaj had chosen to let the dress stand alone, without a jacket or trousers, as one would otherwise see at the fashion show.

ZOË KRAVITZ
"YSL HAS ALWAYS BEEN ONE OF MY FAVORITE BRANDS. IT'S TIMELESS AND EFFORT-LESSLY COOL."

Zoë Kravitz

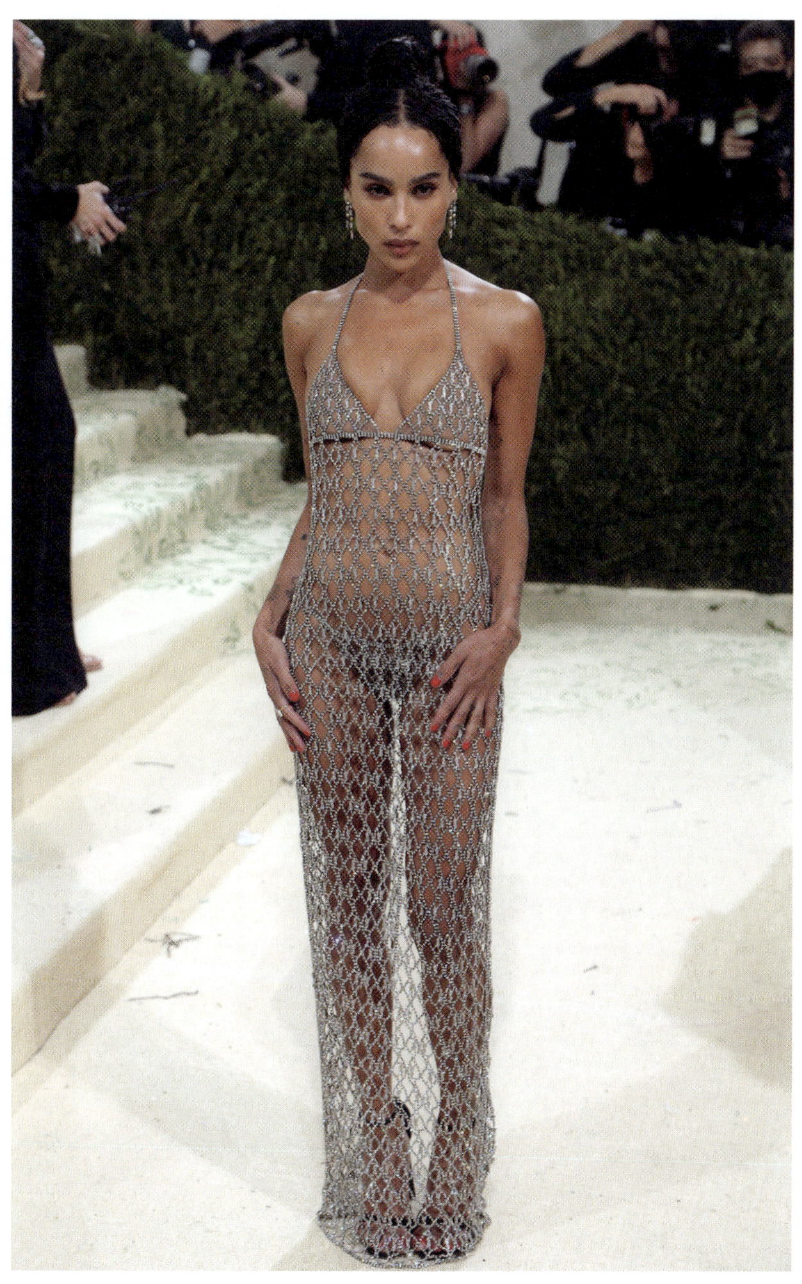

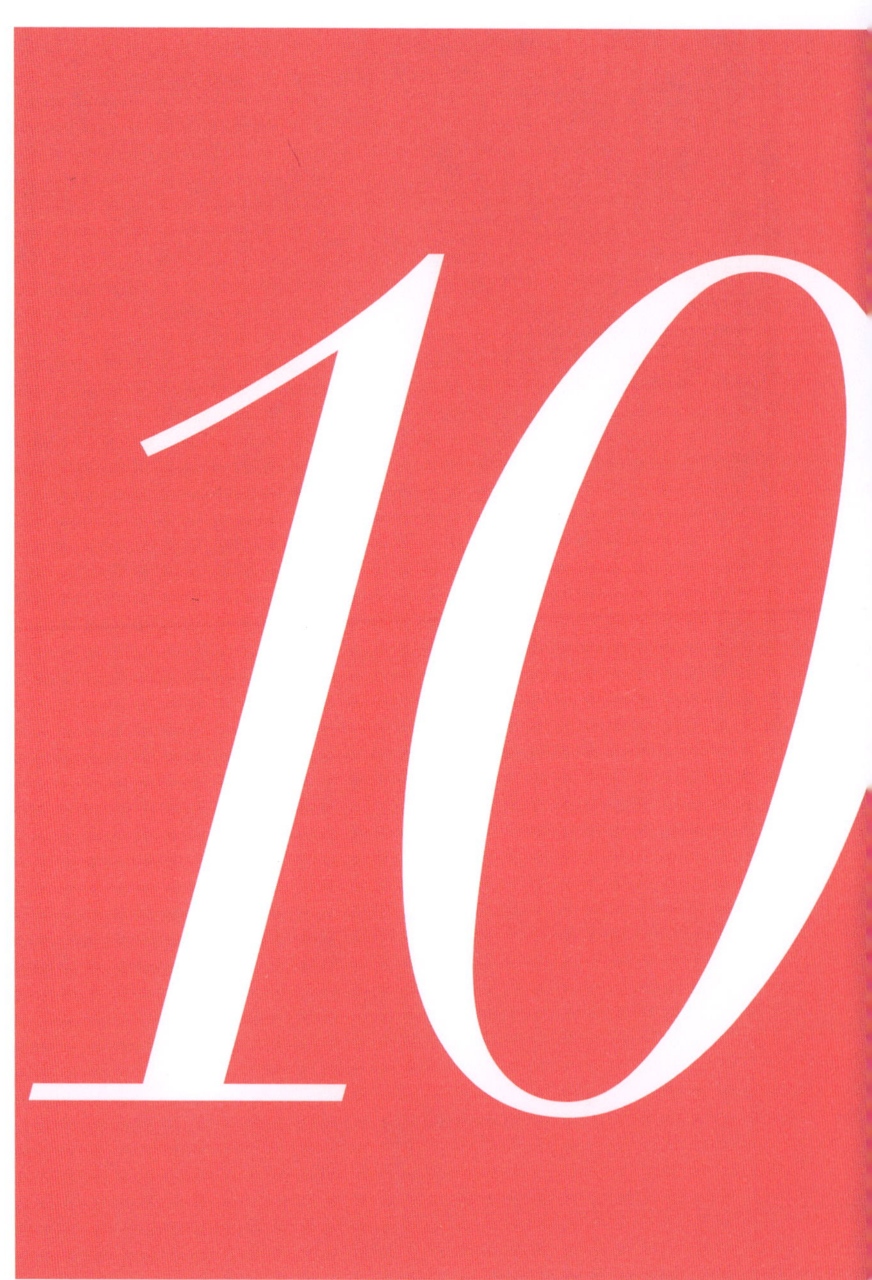

HOW YSL WILL TACKLE *the* NEXT ERA

The Future

Anthony Vaccarello has been the House of Yves Saint Laurent's creative director since 2016 and seems quite happy to lead the fashion juggernaut into the next era. Plus, under the parent company Kering, the company is in very capable corporate hands. The last reported global revenue for YSL was around $3 billion in 2023. The company's headquarters remain on the Rue de Bellechasse in Paris, France.

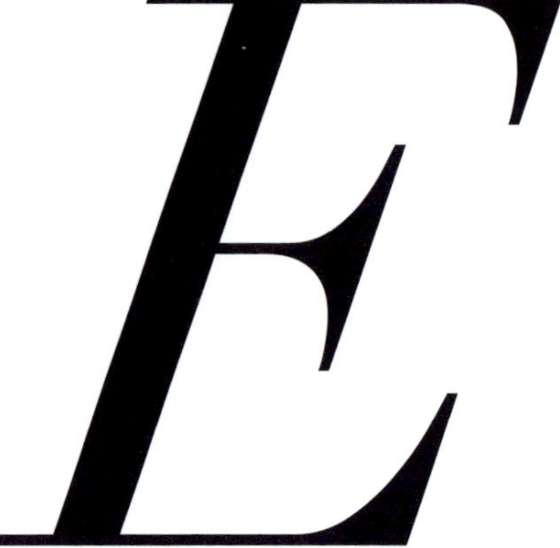

ven though YSL has been around since the '60s and its creator Yves Saint Laurent passed away in 2008, the brand is on solid footing. With its ready-to-wear line, haute couture, accessories, and beauty products all maintaining the luxury allure that everyone loves, it's clear that YSL has a bright future. The company is always looking for ways to help the environment, champion diversity, and work on new projects.

One of the newest projects for 2024 is a film production company called Saint Laurent Productions. Anthony Vaccarello is leading the team on this one and has been getting A-list directors to make films. The company has produced three long feature films that will be shown at the Cannes Film Festival in May 2024: Emilia Perez, by Jacques Audiard; Parthenope, by Paolo Sorrentino; and The Shrouds, by David Cronenberg. This is the first time a luxury design house has helmed film projects. It's truly an inspired way to take YSL into the future in a completely different way. The costuming for each film is by Anthony Vaccarello. The actors starring in the films include Zoe Saldana, Selena Gomez, Diane Krugar, Edgar Ramirez, and Guy Pearce. Hollywood's A-list is obviously interested in being part of this new endeavor for Saint Laurent.

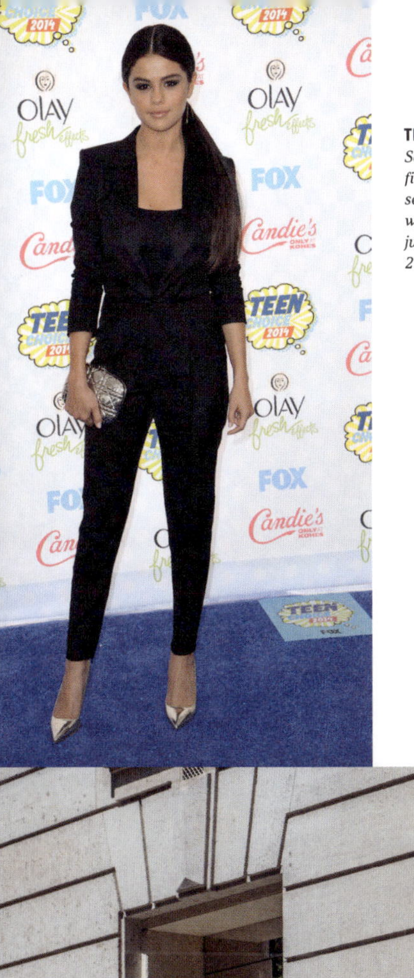

THE BIG SCREEN

Selena Gomez stars in the YSL film Emilia Perez. Here she is seen at the Teen Choice Awards wearing a tailored tuxedo jumpsuit from the Spring/Summer 2014 YSL collection.

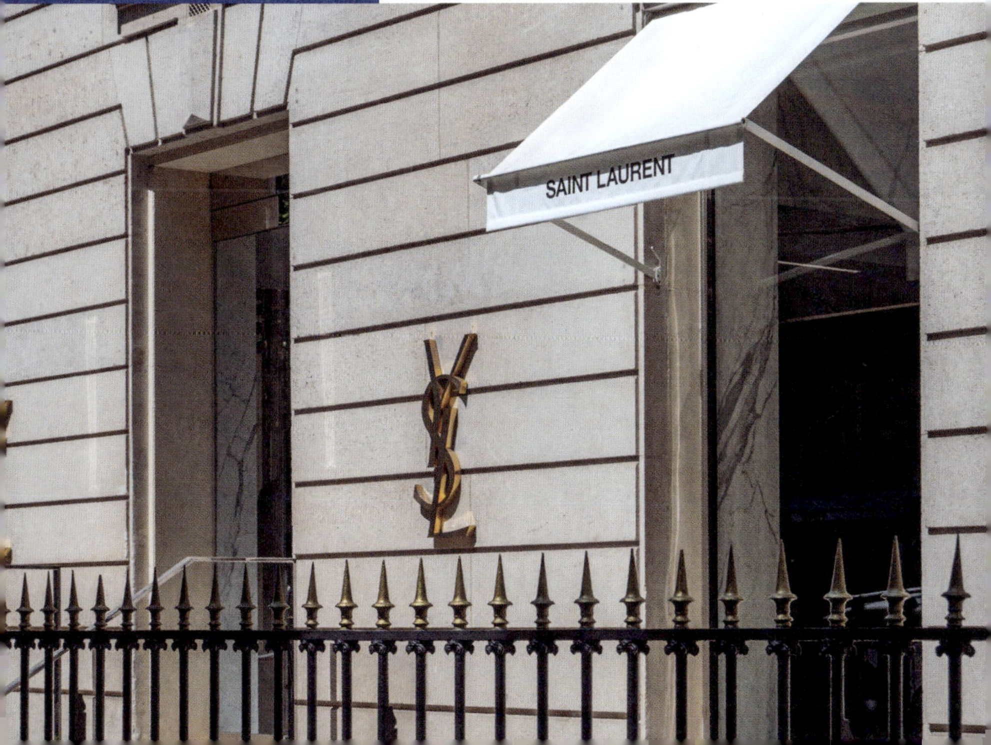

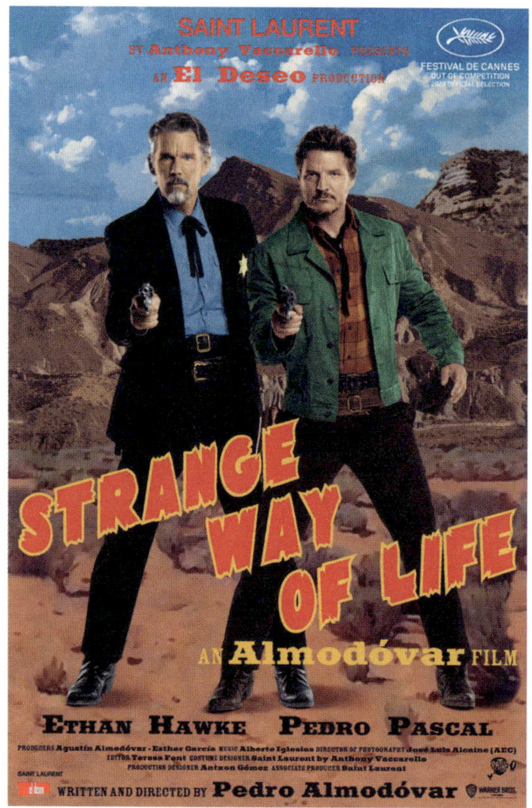

The production company worked on short features last year. One of the first films it made was a short film by Pedro Almodovar called Strange Way of Life. It starred Ethan Hawke and Pedro Pascal as cowboys with an interesting past, and the costuming in this film was all Saint Laurent by Anthony Vaccarello. It was shown at the 2023 Cannes Film Festival before it had a wider release in mainstream theaters, and it can currently be streamed online on Netflix.

Apart from filmmaking, sustainability is always on the mind of everyone involved in YSL. The fashion house is constantly working on ways to improve the lives of the workers in its supply chain, implement responsible sourcing, and decrease the company's carbon footprint.

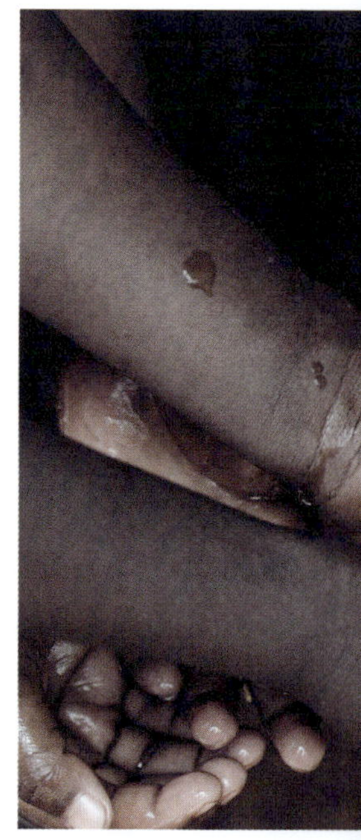

One of the biggest charitable drives YSL has launched is a clean water initiative in partnership with the nonprofit organization charity: water, which aims to end the global water crisis. With its founder, Scott Harrison, the charity has helped bring clean water to developing countries since 2017. It has founded nearly 40 projects in countries such as Ethiopia, India, and Malawi, helping more than 8,000 people. These projects primarily involve building sustainable water systems that can provide clean and safe drinking water in rural areas.

In the fashion world, YSL continues to push the boundaries with everything it does. The Fall 2024 Collection featured a variety of sheer materials in all kinds of colors, including tan, midnight blue, and emerald green. Anthony Vaccarello's singular vision to create these looks in similar silhouettes was simultaneously breathtakingly elegant and sexy. The collection was impossibly chic against the backdrop of the Eiffel Tower in Paris. It will be exciting to see what this glorious fashion house will do in the future.

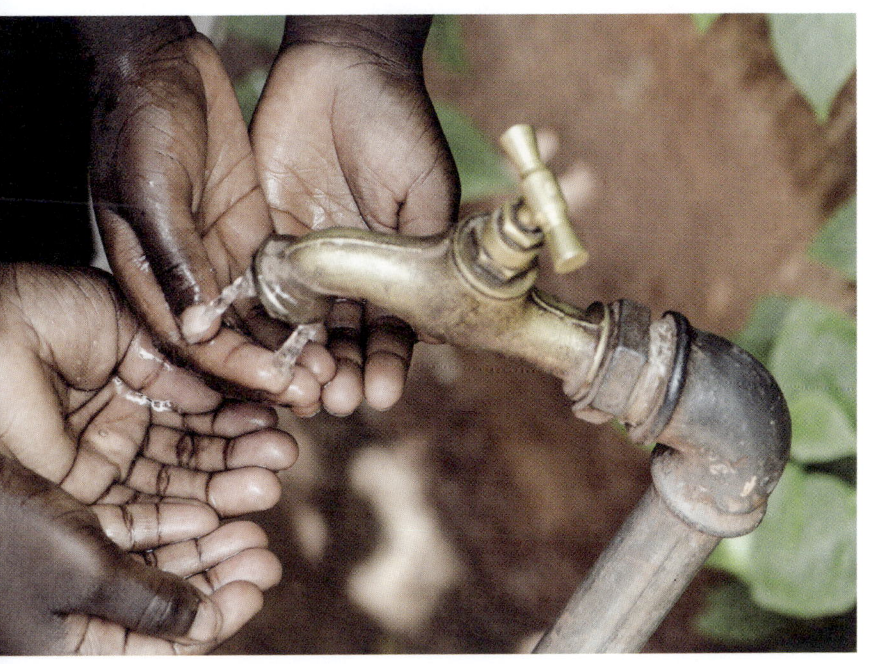

“FASHIONS FADE; *STYLE IS ETERNAL.*”

Yves Saint Laurent

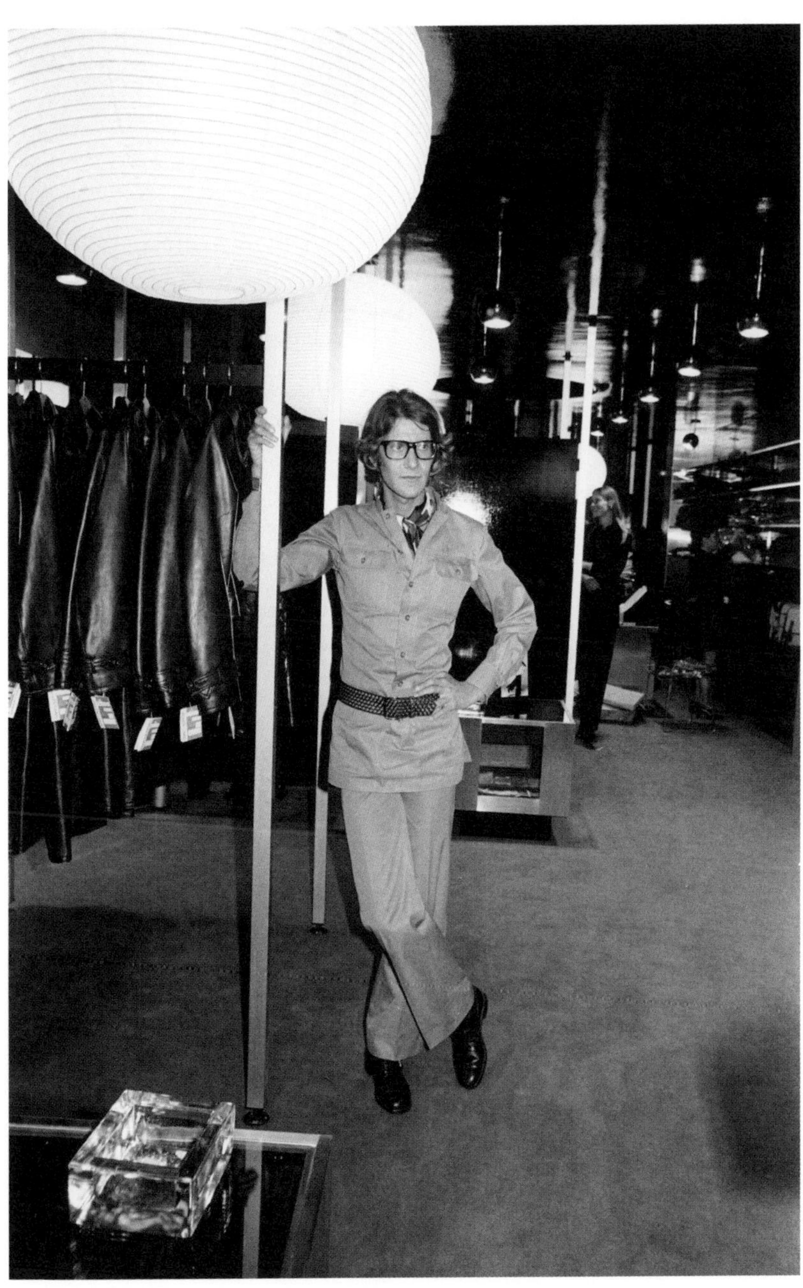

CREDITS

Helmin & Sorgenfri would like to thank the following for permission to use images in this book.

Keystone Press	Alamy Stock Photo	6
Trinity MirrorMirrorpix	Alamy Stock Photo	7
Keystone Press	Alamy Stock Photo	8
Valentina	Linnik	10
Album	Alamy Stock Photo	11
firstVIEW		12
Keystone Press	Alamy Stock Photo	15
firstVIEW		18
firstVIEW		19
Abaca Press	Alamy Stock Photo	19
Abaca Press	Alamy Stock Photo	20
Valentina Linnik		21
Abaca Press	Alamy Stock Photo	23
UPI	Alamy Stock Photo	24
WENN Rights Ltd	Alamy Stock Photo	27
f11photo	Shutterstock.com	30
frederic REGLAIN	Alamy Stock Photo	32
Keystone Press	Alamy Stock Photo	33
Valentina	Linnik	35
humphery	Shutterstock.com	36
Abaca Press	Alamy Stock Photo	37
wayne Tippetts	Alamy Stock Photo	38/39
Featureflash	Dreamstime.com	41
Moviestore Collection Ltd	Alamy Stock Photo	45
AGIP	Bridgeman Images	46
firstVIEW		46
ZUMA Press, Inc.	Alamy Stock Photo	47
Roman Belogorodov	Dreamstime.com	48
firstVIEW		50
firstVIEW		52/53
firstVIEW		54
firstVIEW		55
Trinity MirrorMirrorpix	Alamy Stock Photo	57
Neydtstock	Dreamstime.com	60
Creative Lab	Shutterstock.com	61
Valentina Linnik		62
Sorbis	Shutterstock.com	63
photo-lime	Shutterstock.com	64

NeydtStock	Shutterstock.com	65
firstVIEW		66
Albertophotography	Dreamstime.com	68
Zhi Qi	Dreamstime.com	70
Starstock	Dreamstime.com	73
Valentina Linnik		76
Trinity MirrorMirrorpix	Alamy Stock Photo	77
Image Press Agency	Alamy Stock Photo	79
NeydtStock	Shutterstock.com	80
KPad	Shutterstock.com	81
Yau Ming Low	Shutterstock.com	83
Sorbis	Shutterstock.com	84/85
Olga_Berezhna	Shutterstock.com	86
Grzegorz Czapski	Alamy Stock Photo	87
snaziihah	Shutterstock.com	89
lev radin	Shutterstock.com	91
Alamy.com		94
NICKY1841	Shutterstock.com	95
NeydtStock	Shutterstock.com	96
Tea	Dreamstime.com	99
Maria Rom	Shutterstock.com	100
Antonina Babchenko	Shutterstock.com	101
Ilsur Nigmatzyanov	Dreamstime.com	102
Ilsur Nigmatzyanov	Dreamstime.com	105
Ovidiu Hrubaru	Shutterstock.com	106
firstVIEW		111
Loredana Sangiuliano	Shutterstock.com	112
Retro AdArchives	Alamy Stock Photo	113
Sipa USA	Alamy Stock Photo	115
Featureflash	Dreamstime.com	116
ZUMA Press, Inc.	Alamy Stock Photo	118
Jennifer Graylock	Alamy Stock Photo	119
INTERFOTO	Alamy Stock Photo	121
BAKOUNINE	Shutterstock.com	125
WENN Rights Ltd	Alamy Stock Photo	126
Suzan Moore	Alamy Stock Photo	128
MediaPunch Inc	Alamy Stock Photo	129
ZUMA Press, Inc.	Alamy Stock Photo	130
Jaguarps	Dreamstime.com	131
Abaca Press	Alamy Stock Photo	133
Jaguar PS	Shutterstock.com	136
Hcazenave	Dreamstime.com	136
Entertainment Pictures	Alamy Stock Photo	138
Riccardo Mayer	Shutterstock.com	139
Trinity MirrorMirrorpix	Alamy Stock Photo	141

Published in 2024 by Helmin & Sorgenfri
Nivå Strandpark 21, 1
DK-2990 Nivå
Denmark

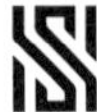

TEXT: Kelly Reising
DESIGN: butter am brot / Morten Svendsen

ISBN: 978-87-94190-60-2

Printed in EU
1. edition, 1. printing

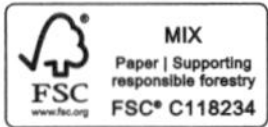